spiritual realities

Volume 5

SPIRITUAL DYNAMICS BETWEEN PEOPLE

by
Harold R. Eberle

Winepress Publishing
Yakima, Washington, USA

Spiritual Realities, Volume V:
Spiritual Dynamics Between People

© 1998 by Harold R. Eberle

Winepress Publishing
P.O. Box 10653
Yakima, WA 98909-1653
1-800-308-5837
(509-248-5837 from outside the USA)

Library of Congress Catalog Card No. 97-060374
ISBN 1-882523-13-X

Cover by Jeff Boettcher
Graphic Art by Eugene M. Holmes

All biblical quotations are taken from the *New American Standard Bible* © 1977, The Lockman Foundation, La Habra, California 90631.

Printed in the United States of America

Dedication and Thanks

This book would not have been possible if it had not been for Pastor Jim Leuschen of Spokane, Washington, who helped me think through the many doctrinal issues and challenged me on numerous points. His theological insight brought me back down to earth and forced me to communicate spiritual principles in understandable terms.

Also, I had input and editing advice from Pastor Peter Eisenmann, Steve Marusic, Dennis Jacobson, Greg Wilkinson, and Annette Bradley. Each of these have left their mark on these pages.

Table Of Contents

Introduction

The soul of man remains superimposed upon and associated with the physical body. The spirit, however, is not limited to the confines of the body. It originated with the breath of God, and therefore, is not limited to natural laws. This *God stuff* in each of us is the energy which circulates and flows, enabling us to live, think, and influence the world around us.

We established these truths about man's nature in preceding volumes. I refer you back to those writings for fuller understanding.

Our focus in this volume will be upon the dynamics and interaction between people's spirits. Our spirits influence each other. It is eye-opening to see some of these truths revealed both in the Bible and in present-day experiences.

1

Becoming of One Accord and Bonding

There are specific properties of the human spirit which we can identify and discuss. Understanding these properties will give great insight into human behavior and the spiritual dynamics between people.

For example, we find in the New Testament that the disciples became *of one accord* on several occasions (e.g., Acts 4:24; 5:12). As they became of one accord, they had their hearts oriented toward each other to such an extent that they were selling their personal properties and holding all possessions in common (e.g., Acts 2:44-45; 4:32). Both their desires and their thoughts were in agreement.

This property of the human spirit to become of one accord with others is key in understanding human behavior. It happens when people orient their hearts toward each other or toward a common goal.

We can obtain further understanding of this truth by examining the words of our Lord Jesus when He explained how two or more believers can come into agreement with each other (Matt. 18:19). The *agreement* of which He spoke is more than two people merely coming into a mental assent or people showing an outer form of unity. The Greek word which has been interpreted *agreement*, is *sumphoneo* (from which we get the word symphony). This Greek word often is used in reference to musical instruments being made to sound in one accord or in harmony. In this fashion, just as musical instruments can come into harmony, so also can two or more people harmonize spiritually.

In order to develop a mental picture of what is taking place spiritually as two people come into agreement, envision two similar musical tuning forks. If one is struck so it begins vibrating, it will send off a specific tone. If the second tuning fork is moved close to the vibrating one, soon it too will begin to vibrate at the same frequency.

In similar fashion, the human spirit has the ability to become of one accord with the spirits of those around. To borrow from the specialized vocabulary of sound production, we could say they *become of the same frequency, get on the same wavelength*, or *come into harmony with one another.*

To some readers this vocabulary may sound too mystical for their comfort or too much like terminology used by those involved with New Age thinking. Please do not think that. Remember, we are attempting to understand phenomena which took place in the Bible, and hence, principles which work in relationships between people today.

The Apostle Paul used the term *harmony* when warning Christians not to become united too closely with evil people, giving themselves over to idols:

> Do not be bound together with unbelievers....What *harmony* has Christ with Belial, or what has a believer in common with an unbeliever? (II Cor. 6:14-15, emphasis added).

We examined this passage in Volume II, Chapter 6, and saw how the Christian's spirit actually can become defiled if and when he comes into harmony with those giving themselves over to sin.

What we want to identify here is how people can come into agreement, one accord, or harmony with others; and how this phenomenon involves their entire being, including their spirits.

7

It is the orientation of the heart which determines with whom a person will come into harmony. (I assume the reader understands I am not referring to the muscle that pumps our blood). We use the term *phrone* (pronounced frō nā; Vol. 4, Chapter 12) to refer to the orientation of a person's inner heart. As Proverbs 4:23 tells us, from the heart flow all the issues of life. Because the heart is the core or center from which our spiritual life flows, it determines with whom we will be in tune. As any two or more people *phrone* their hearts in unison, they will come into agreement and unity.

Next, we will add to our understanding of the human spirit how two or more people may become *bonded* to one another. As we discuss this, keep it separated in your mind from the act of becoming of one accord. Later, we will learn how these two spiritual phenomena may take place simultaneously; however, we first want to identify these dynamics as distinct in character.

Our first example of bonding can be that which takes place between Christians. We are told in the Bible that all believers are submerged by the Holy Spirit into one Body (I Cor. 12:12-13). We are united in the spiritual dimension. When one part hurts, we all hurt; as one is blessed, we are all partakers of that blessing (I Cor. 12:26). Our spirits are bonded in such a fashion that they influence each other, both positively and negatively. This is the way God made us.

People also are bonded together in the marriage relationship: "two become one." These words are not merely figures of speech, but should be taken in a deep and very real sense. As married people point their hearts toward each other and grow in their commitment to each other, the bonding between them deepens.

Whenever people open their hearts to one another, they may become bonded. Friends become spiritually linked. For example, we are told in First Samuel 18:1 that "...the soul of Jonathan was knit to the soul of David, and Jonathan loved him as himself."

Some Christians call such relationships "soul ties." In an earlier volume, we pointed out that the term "soul tie" can be misleading. When the Bible says, "the soul of Jonathan was knit to the soul of David," it is not implying that the soul of either reached out across space and touched the soul of the other. No. We understand that the soul is limited to the confines of the body (except at death and in certain cases discussed in Volumes IV and VII). Therefore, it is more accurate to see these bonds as spiritual energy emanating from the soul and touching the soul of another. It is spiritual substance which ties the soul of one to the soul of another.

These bonds occur in numerous situations of life. Parents and children bond with one another, and this is good and right. Co-workers unite in heart and, therefore, spiritually as well. Any people who share experiences, especially those experiences demanding commitments, bond to one another, and those associations are real spiritual ties knitting their souls together.

In order to embrace this truth, we must accept that the substance of the human spirit is *cohesive*. We will use this term to explain the property of the human spirit to *stick to, merge with,* or *blend with* the spirits of others.

This property is more than just a *mixing* of two people's spiritual energies. We are attempting to develop a biblical view of how God created man to function. More is involved than the spirits of people *sticking* to each other. The spiritual energy of one actually merges (in the sense of *becoming one*) with the spiritual substance of others. Only if we accept this property can we understand the spiritual dynamics we observe in life and read about in the Bible.

For example, we are told that in the marriage relationship, two become one. Our Lord emphasized this truth by saying, "They are no longer two, but one" (Matt. 19:6).

In the natural world, one plus one always equals two. In the spiritual world that is not necessarily so. When speaking of the merging of spiritual energies, one plus one can equal one. We are not talking just about joining or adding, but a supernatural—spiritual—merging.

It is in this fashion that we understand all spiritual bonding takes place.

We explained such merging in Volume II, Chapter 5, when discussing the merging of God's Spirit with the believer's spirit. The Apostle Paul explained: "But the one who joins himself to the Lord is one spirit with Him" (I Cor. 6:17). The example we gave in that earlier discussion was how a certain tribe of people express their love for one another, not by kissing, but by a man and a woman inhaling each other's breath. That is a powerful picture of the spirits of two people intermingling and being taken within. Similarly, when the Christian is united with God, their spirits are no longer two, but one.

The depth of merging between two people is determined by the depth of heart commitment. The strength of the bond is the result of individuals pointing their hearts toward each other. As they work together, they increase their unity. As they go through trials and difficulties, their hearts must be more fixed and stable. Each time a problem arises, they each must make a decision whether to remain together or split and go their independent ways. Therefore, every project, trial, or stress is an opportunity for people to deepen the spiritual bonding between them.

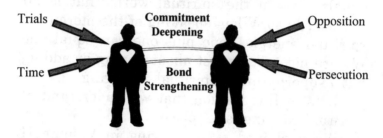

When speaking of open commitments between two or more people, we sometimes use the term *covenant relationships.* In some Christian circles these terms have been abused, and people have been coerced into abusive relationships. Here we are not referring to any manipulative, controlling type of bonds between people. Rather, we simply are speaking of deep levels of commitment which all people form at various times during their lives. Those commitments may have been formed through spoken words, long periods of time together, or just investments by those involved which demand great sacrifices. Covenants made openly and in the depths of people's hearts establish spiritual forces that influence every person's life. We will see profound implications from covenant relationships in the following chapters, but first we want to explain another spiritual dynamic occurring between people.

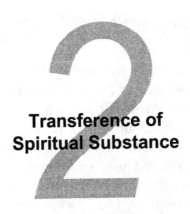

Transference of
Spiritual Substance

Not only is it possible for people to come into harmony and to bond with others, but there is also the possibility for a transference of spiritual energy to move from one person to another. These three spiritual dynamics may happen simultaneously, but here let's focus on the transference of spiritual substance between people.

Looking again in the Bible, we can read about a woman with a hemorrhage who pressed through a crowd in order to touch the hem of Jesus' garment. Our Lord turned and asked who had touched Him, for He was aware that power or virtue had flowed out of Him (Luke 8:43-48). What we want to identify here is the invisible, spiritual substance or energy that moved out of Jesus and into this woman.

For another example, we can read how Elijah's spirit was transmitted to his disciple Elisha (II Kings 2:7-25). Before Elijah was taken up into heaven, Elisha asked him, "Please, let a double portion of your spirit be upon me" (II Kings 2:9).

Elijah responded by saying that Elisha would have his request if he saw him being taken up into heaven. After Elijah was taken from this earth, the other prophets noted, "The spirit of Elijah rests on Elisha" (II Kings 2:15).

As we study these examples, it is important for us to recognize what was actually being transmitted between people. Was it the Holy Spirit or was it the human spirit? In the example of Elijah and Elisha, the Bible tells us that it was the "*spirit of Elijah*" that came upon Elisha (II Kings 2:15). Some Christians would try to explain away this phenomenon, thinking that only the Holy Spirit could have been transferred; however, I challenge you to accept this Bible passage literally. Two different times we are told that it was "the spirit of Elijah."

At this point, we must distinguish between the spirit and the soul of a person. For further clarification on this, I refer you back to Volume II, Chapters 1 and 2. It is not the soul which is transmitted between people. Otherwise we would be giving credence to a form of reincarnation—which we *definitely are not*. Please do not misunderstand. If we are going to take the Bible literally, then we must recognize that the spiritual energy which was in Elijah, to some degree, was passed on into Elisha. However, this does not mean that Elijah's soul was transmitted.

We also understand that God's Spirit was upon Elijah. God's Spirit and Elijah's spirit were bonded together. Therefore, the spiritual sub-

14

stance which flowed out of him and into Elisha was a portion of his spirit and the anointing of God upon his life.

In the following examples, we will not spend much time discerning what spirit is being transmitted. Here we simply want to establish the principle of how the spiritual life-energies resident within a person can be drawn out and deposited in another individual. Whatever spiritual energy is within a person, good or bad, it can be passed on.

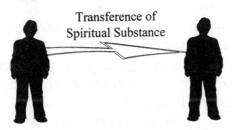

Transference of
Spiritual Substance

The most dramatic exchange occurs within marriage. Not only do a man and a woman bond, but the life-energies in one actually go into the other. The more time two people spend with one another, opening up their hearts to each other, the greater this transfer of life will become.

In the family, children draw upon the spiritual energy of their parents. In a church, the preacher influences his congregation not only with his teaching, but also with the spirit flowing through him. Every leader transmits spiritual substance to his followers. The coach transmits his energy to his team. The famous musician releases his spirit along with his voice, and people receive his spirit as they are bathed with his words. Any person with authority emanates spiritual energy, and others who submit to it may actually receive it within themselves.

As the spiritual substance of one person is incorporated into the life of another, the second person will take on certain characteristics of the first. Their thoughts and desires become similar. Jesus said that a pupil becomes like his teacher (Luke 6:40). Followers receive the nature of those they admire.

Often this spiritual transfer has a negative influence in the life of the receiver. For example, some parents have watched their children make dramatic shifts in their personality and behavior after being exposed to some famous rock musician. A certain teenager may be doing well in school and living in harmony at home, but then, after attending a huge concert, suddenly becomes rebellious toward authority. Their priorities and attitudes may change. They no longer enjoy school, and they crave more exposure to the same negative crowd of people. We can explain such radical changes as we recognize the spiritual principles involved. Spiritual transmissions can occur easily as a young person idolizes, submits to, and longs for whatever he sees in the new-found idol.

In the Bible, we are told that "bad company corrupts good morals" (I Cor. 15:33). To see how such corruption can be the result of spiritual transfers, read Second Corinthians 6:14-7:1. In chapter seven, verse one, Paul told the Christians to cleanse themselves from all "defilement of flesh and spirit." The five verses preceding this one reveal to us how such defilement can happen through our bonding with people who worship idols, commit fornication, or give themselves to other sins (this is explained fully in Volume II, Chapter 6). Similarly, we can read in First Corinthians 5:1-6 where Paul explained how the evil influence of a sexually perverted man could spread to everyone bonded to him, in the same fashion that yeast spreads and leavens a whole lump of dough. From such passages, we can recognize how the transfer of spiritual substance can influence the thoughts and behaviors of those who receive it.

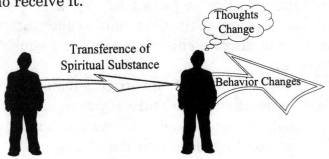

Thoughts Change

Transference of Spiritual Substance

Behavior Changes

Likewise, we also must recognize the *good* transfers of spiritual energy. For example, when a young boy admires and associates with his father, there are forces activated which mold that son's character. When a daughter spends quality time with her mother, that daughter is being bonded to and molded more to her image. Through a Christian perspective, we can explain this phenomenon and say that all people have an invisible side to their being, and the spirit/soul of each person is influenced by the relationships he or she has.

Not only are the thoughts and desires of a person changed through such transfers, but *authority, wisdom,* and *blessings* also can be transmitted. When Elisha received the spirit of Elijah, he received an anointing and empowering upon his life similar to what Elijah had. God told Moses to lay his hands upon Joshua so that his *authority* would be transferred (Num. 27:20). Amazingly, Joshua received not only authority from Moses but also *wisdom* (Deut 34:9). It was a common practice in Bible times for a person of known stature to lay his hands upon others, especially his own children, to pass blessings on to them.

This truth—that spiritual substance can carry with it some measure of *power, authority, wisdom,* and/or *blessing*—is eye-opening, challenging, exciting, hope-creating...!

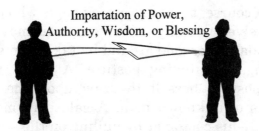

Impartation of Power, Authority, Wisdom, or Blessing

When such a *transference* is made, we use the term *impartation*. An impartation is a transference in which some measure of power, authority, wisdom, and/or blessing moves with the spiritual substance between people.

We also can identify at this point how people actually *draw out* spiritual substance from another person. The woman who touched the hem of Jesus' garment was submissive and longing. Similarly, a person must submit to or "get under" their leader if they hope to receive his spiritual strength, authority, or wisdom. It is as if they are tipping a glass of water to flow *downward* toward them. Also, they must have an openness and desire to receive that which is pouring forth.

People posture themselves in different ways to receive different things. A daughter finds a specific manner in which to draw upon her father's love. A wife discovers a different place from which she relates to her husband. An employee approaches his boss in one way, and he will speak to his fellow workers in another manner. Friends posture themselves in specific ways toward each other, and those manners may change from time to time.

Of course, there are some people who posture themselves wrongly. A certain man may try to intimidate everyone around by taking on a domineering, threatening posture. A lonely woman may posture herself to draw upon the sexual desires of unknown men. A salesman may manipulate his customer by pulling on the strings of his or her heart. Individuals raised in an environment with very little affection, constantly may yearn for the acceptance of others.

Self-pity is a negative force in these respects. Through self-pity a person wrongfully draws on the spiritual energy of those around him. Self-pity is the positioning of one's soul in a selfish manner, which draws in—or steals—the energy of other people around. It is a form of lust for or coveting of other people's strength and love. Some people develop a lifestyle of self-pity, and they drain the energy of everyone who comes around them. Of course, there are needy people to whom we must give special attention, but the pattern of life which wrongly pulls on the spiritual energy of other people should not be encouraged.

Drawing in Spiritual Substance of Others

In coming pages, we will see many more situations in which spiritual transfers are made. At this point, we can recognize that transfers take place as people bond with each other and as individuals longingly look up to some leader. The more people open their hearts and receive, the more they will be changed by the resulting transfer of spiritual energy.

Although we are not always aware of these spiritual dynamics, they are evident in the world around us. Most of us are consciously or subconsciously aware of energy moving between us, but we seldom have the opportunity to discuss these realities. More importantly, we Christians have not been taught a biblical basis for understanding spiritual dynamics. As a result, we rarely have communicated about them, even though the transfer of spiritual life between us is real, and every one of us experiences it every day of our lives.

3

The Giver of
Spiritual Substance

We have studied how spiritual substance can be transferred from one person to another, and how that may result in a change in the recipient. Now, let's turn our attention to the giver and see what effect there is upon his mind, emotions, and behavior.

As spiritual energy flows from a person's innermost being, that energy influences his thoughts. Remember that "the spirit of a man reveals the thoughts of a man." As the spiritual energy flows, it also stimulates certain emotions, desires, and strengths.

Even the physical body of a person may be energized. Therefore, as followers believe in and pull on their leader in a healthy way, the resulting increased flow of energy through him may energize his soul and body in numerous and varied ways.

Because of these dynamics, the football hero performs his best when the crowds cheer. The pastor can know the direction of God for his congregation as the hearts of the people look to him. A man can lead better in his own home when his family is looking to him for direction. It is easier for the army general to make brilliant decisions if his men believe in him. The president is more effective if his country supports him. The foreman on a construction site will have more energy and creative ideas if the men working for him have respect for his position and for who he is.

People who often appear before large crowds become sensitive to these principles. They may not understand that it is spiritual energy being released, but they commonly realize that the people must draw upon them before they can function at their best. Actors and public speakers know that they cannot effectively communicate until the listeners are waiting expectantly for them to speak. A hostile or bored crowd is a difficult group before whom to perform, and a great output of inner energy is demanded. A minister typically finds it much easier to bring forth his message in front of an eager congregation. The hunger and desire of the people draw the spiritual energy out of the person at the front. As the energy flows through the leader, it is easier for him to think, act in boldness, and speak with authority.

That which is pulled from a leader is *a specific flow* of spiritual energy. It is as if a stream begins to flow out through the person and quickens their thoughts in the related area. That area may be knowledge for a specific endeavor or strength to accomplish some task. Sometimes Christian leaders find themselves receiving incredible revelation, that is, inspired understanding, as they are standing before needy people. Comedians depend upon a specific stream being pulled out of them by those listening; the stream that is released quickens their own thoughts, giving them cute things to say, fast responses, and unusual ways of looking at life. In my own work as an author, I find that I cannot write effectively unless I expose myself to the people for whom I am writing, and keep them in mind and heart as I write. Similarly, inventors, scientists, and people doing research in various areas very often are dependent upon the needs of those around them to draw out of them the spiritual energy they need to formulate answers. In all such cases, it is a specific stream of spiritual energy being pulled out of their innermost being and through their mind.

The flow of spiritual energy through a person or into a person normally is healthy and it feels good. The mother holding her child senses the love flowing out of her, and this creates a sense of warmth and significance. When a daughter acts cute for her father, both usually are enjoying the interaction. As a young man and woman look romantically into each other's eyes, there is a pleasurable sensation that we usually call "falling in love." As people pull on the athlete to perform, he feels energized and powerful. The strong leader directing a large crowd is aware of confidence and energy stirring within him. He may feel a rush of energy through his entire being. Some actors and musicians are even known to get "addicted to the rush." Having other people pull on one's spirit can be a very rewarding or even pleasurable experience.

Sometimes, however, people can pull energy out of an individual wrongfully, resulting in harmful effects. Just as the physical body can become exhausted, so also can the spirit of a person. Several Bible verses talk about the spirit of a person being depleted, crushed, or oppressed (e.g., I Sam 1:15; Ps. 142:3; Prov. 15:4). In some cases, this may be the result of negative interactions between people.

People can be so longing for the direction and strength of their leader that they "drain" his spiritual energy. This can happen just as easily in the life of the minister as it can with the mother who cares for her children. Because the human spirit can be drained away and weakened in this way, wise leaders consciously keep enough energy to maintain themselves and stay strong.

Some givers are not aware of these dynamics, and they allow others to take too much of their spiritual energy. They can become so depleted that they do not have enough energy left within themselves to maintain their own well-being. Physical illness can result. It may become difficult for them to keep healthy thought patterns, and they may lose all motivation to live. Often, Christians fall into this because, in their earnestness to do good, they force themselves to help others beyond what is right. Guilt, too, can become a trap holding or causing people to drain themselves on behalf of others.

As we mentioned in the last chapter, self-pity is the posturing of one's soul to lust or covet after the strength of others. If the giver does not want to give of his or her spiritual energy, then he or she will feel robbed. His or her strength will decrease.

We also can see spiritual strength being taken from individuals when we observe certain relationships between men and women. When a young man looks longingly at a beautiful woman, he may draw upon her spiritual energy. If she is uninterested in him, she may have a true sensation that he is stealing from her. If, however, she desires a relationship with him, she will find his glance appealing and pleasurable. What makes the experience pleasurable or not for her, depends upon her heart and whether or not she desires his attention.

What we discover is that spiritual energy seems to be *reproduced* in the giver if it is willingly given. On the other hand, it is diminished if stolen. This principle is such an important key, allow me to explain it another way.

Spiritual energy has an incredible living, reproductive nature. Remember, it originated with God. It is not natural in its essence, but is from the very breath of God. Realizing this, we can understand more easily its properties within man. When it is stolen, that is, when a person's heart is not directed toward the *taker*, the amount of available spiritual energy will be depleted. If, however, the giver wants to give, the spiritual energy seems to reproduce itself. The more that is given, the more that grows. An amount may be released from a certain person, and yet the same amount or more remains in that person. Spiritual energy is creative in this sense, and when it is allowed to flow in the direction one's heart is pointed, it then reproduces itself in others and in the giver.

When spiritual energy is being transmitted between two people in a healthy manner, it usually will be an enjoyable, refreshing experience for both. Of course, there are times we must give unselfishly and pour out ourselves for others. But generally speaking, a healthy exchange of spiritual energy is a good, wholesome part of life.

4

Conditions for Spiritual Exchanges

Thus far, we have identified specific spiritual dynamics between people and several properties of the human spirit. Allow me to list them below for clarification.

Spiritual Dynamics Between People
1. Becoming of one accord or coming into harmony
2. Bonding
3. Transference of spiritual substance

Properties of the Human Spirit
1. May harmonize with that which surrounds it
2. Cohesive or able to mingle whereby the energies of two become one
3. Reproductive, re-creative, or able to multiply itself.

Now, let's discuss when and under what conditions spiritual dynamics between people are most evident.

Remember that the heart of man is the fountainhead of his being (Prov. 4:23). Therefore, whenever two or more people expose their hearts to each other, they are opening the doorways of their hearts for harmonizing, bonding, and spiritual transfers.

For this reason, heart-to-heart, open communication is a spiritual exercise. When a man and a woman share their deepest feelings with each other, they are bonding. When two friends meet for a cup of coffee and a chat, they are exchanging more than stories with each other. When a public speaker exposes his or her heart, everyone who is listening likely will be influenced by his or her spirit.

If people hold up the walls of their hearts against each other, then transfers and bonding are hindered or completely stopped. However, as individuals relax and allow themselves to trust each other, the doorways for transfers are opened.

For this reason, eating a meal with another person increases spiritual exchanges. There is something about eating which tends to relax people—not a formal meal, but a less tense time when people enjoy each other's company and communicate openly. They typically let down their guard and expose themselves more freely.

Laughter can crumble further the walls that divide. Every public speaker knows that he will be able to communicate more effectively with an audience if he can loosen up the crowd with a joke or two. College roommates who find themselves laughing together uncontrollably, will be bonded for life. Consciously or subconsciously, people sense that they are bonding every time they laugh unhindered with others.

It is not only the laughing, but *the losing control* that opens the door for transfers. When individuals release their inhibitions, they usually are lowering their inner walls.

Because of this, people who drink alcohol together often bond with each other. Alcohol and certain other drugs remove walls. People who smoke marijuana or experiment with hallucinogenic drugs together typically form deep bonds.

Conditions of losing control happen in numerous other, more acceptable, situations of life, as well. For example, when two men are watching a televised football game, they may become so absorbed in the excitement and intensity that they shout, laugh, and abandon all restraint. When a woman cries at the theater, she is losing control and may be yielding her heart to the person with her. When a father and son wrestle playfully in the living room of their home, they may be having such fun that the walls completely fall and bonding is activated.

Similarly, the sight of something beautiful can cause a person to lose control of himself or herself. For example, when a man and a woman gaze at a sunset together, they may be releasing strong forces which are bonding them as one. As a man is captivated by the beauty of his wife, his spirit is harmonizing with hers.

Notice, a difference between bonding and harmonizing. A married couple are bonded because of years together. However, they may find themselves not in harmony with one another from time to time. They still will be deeply bonded to each other, but because their hearts have been oriented differently, they may get out of harmony. Perhaps his heart has been *phroneated* toward his work for an extended period, and she has been focused on her own career or their children. Because of this, they may be out of sync, or on two different wavelengths. Therefore, when they come together they may find it difficult to communicate with each other. They love each other and have years of bonding, yet the condition of harmonizing is a much more immediate, short-term condition.

A husband and wife who find themselves out of sync with each other can get back on the same wavelength by orienting their hearts in the same direction. The best thing for them to do is avoid arguing and focusing directly on each other. That normally causes greater conflict. They can get on the same wavelength much easier by *phroneating* in the same direction. Doing things such as going to watch a movie together, enjoying a relaxed meal, or sitting on the porch of their home and looking at the stars can help bring them back into harmony. Any time two or more people point their affections and attention toward the same focal point, strong forces are activated to bring them into harmony.

Parents who understand these principles more effectively can reach a child who seems distant or estranged. The way to reach that child *is not* to attack or forcefully demand that they fall into submission. Instead, the parent can determine where their child's heart is pointed and allow the child to talk about that interest. Christian parents often have difficulty with this, because their estranged child may have his or her heart directed toward something of which they disapprove. However, by allowing their child to talk about his or her heart's desire, they are activating the forces of bonding. On the other hand, by forbidding the child to talk about that which has grabbed his or her heart, they are isolating that child.

Similarly, a woman who is trying to win the love of her husband can determine where his heart is pointed and then take steps to orient her heart in the same direction. A man who desires to get on the same wavelength as his wife needs to allow her to talk about the concerns of her heart.

The forces of bonding are especially powerful when two people forget their personal problems, relax, and become still in each other's presence. Therefore, when two people are silently gazing at a sunset, tremendous forces may be working between them. As a family takes a vacation together, they may have several days of being extremely busy and rushing from place to place. There are forces at work during their entire time together, but especially powerful forces will be activated the moment they stop, sit quietly next to each other and say nothing. In that moment, the *individual orientation* of their lives is ceasing, and they are *becoming one.* Energy is being exchanged and thoughts are being aligned. At such moments individual lives may be readjusted and set on common paths.

Similarly, when two people sleep in the same location together, there is typically a bonding that takes place. During sleep people relax and an exchange seems to happen comparable with osmosis.

Sexual intercourse activates even more powerful forces. As two people's passions are aroused the longing within their hearts draws the nature of one into the other. Intercourse is, as we mentioned in Volume I, both a physical and a spiritual experience. In the act, two people detach from the natural realm and focus their affections upon each other. As such, they are open channels to receive the spiritual energy of the other person within themselves.

To various degrees, people become bonded to each other simply by having relationships with one another. Friends become spiritually linked. The Apostle Paul wrote of how he was of "kindred soul" (in Greek: *iso pseuche*; Phil. 2:20) with Timothy. The depth and strength of such bonds vary from one relationship to another.

Authority plays a significant role in forming such bonds. Whenever someone yields to another's authority, he/she may come under that person's spiritual influence. For example, if a police officer rescues a lady in distress, that lady may find herself dreaming about her hero for some time afterward. A husband who provides security for his family will have greater influence in their lives. A pastor who is bold will have a strong influence in the lives of his congregation.

Similarly, the receiving of gifts from another person can be accompanied by the reception of spiritual substance. When money is received as a gift, spiritual strings may be tied. In some cases, when you eat a well-prepared meal, you are yielding to the love, care, and influence of the cook.

When people admire the beauty or skill of some person, they also may come under his/her spiritual influence. Therefore, the singer may sway or influence the crowd not only with his music, but also with his beliefs. An artist may make an impact upon the spirit of the viewer. A gifted writer may draw the reader into a story that captivates the heart and, hence, brings him into his belief system.

Now, all this is not said to put fear into people's lives. We are *not* pointing out these *conditions for transmissions* so that the reader will avoid contact with those around them. Please do not take it that way. Contact with the world around us is inevitable, just as is breathing the same air. There is nothing wrong with enjoying the skills and talents of the people around you. The time we must exercise caution is when evil people are using their gifts and talents to extend their evil purposes.

A time when people are especially receptive to transfers is when they have a spiritual void within them. For example, when a loved one has died, the person left alone easily may reach for a spiritual replacement. Similarly, if a person has gone through the rejection of a close friend, he or she may be left especially vulnerable.

When people reach out in desperation, there may be increased opportunities for transfers. Car accidents, hospital emergencies, and other life-threatening situations may put individuals in a position where he or she reaches out for help and, hence, his or her spirit embraces the touch of another.

There are also certain rhythmic activities which open people spiritually. As we have discussed (Vol. I, Chapter 4), rhythmic music can open people spiritually. Even more powerful is dancing together. So also, when an army marches hour after hour in unison, they are being made to bond as one. When two people walk side by side they may bond—whether it is a man and woman, a father and son, a teacher and disciple, or any other two people. The nature of man is designed in such a manner that when people engage in regular, repeated motion together, they tend to blend as one.

Whenever two or more people go into the realm of the spirit together, spiritual transmissions also may occur spontaneously. We explained in Volume I that *going into the spiritual realm* entails detaching from the natural affairs of life and focusing one's entire attention. Whenever people do this jointly, their spirits are open to receive spiritual substance from each other.

For example, bonding occurs when a group of Christians have a worship service during which they all together direct their hearts toward God. You may observe evidence of such bonding by watching a group of Christians after a church service. They will hang around and fellowship a long time after a service on days that the worship time has been especially captivating and powerful. On the other hand, if God's presence does not seem to be evident during the service, people will leave quickly after everyone is dismissed. For similar reasons, it is difficult for a certain Christian to move away from a city and leave his or her church, if that church regularly has intense times of worship together. An exchange of spiritual life has taken place both among the people and between them and God.

The environment of worship is very similar to the environment of romance that occurs between a man and woman. As a man and woman gaze into each other's eyes over a romantic candlelight dinner, they forget their natural concerns and focus their affections upon each other. In that condition, spiritual bonding easily occurs.

In a worship service where God's presence manifests, it is common not only for transmissions among people, but also for spiritual impartations to occur. In particular, the anointing of the leaders may "leap off them" and be deposited in those who are open to receive. A good example of this is from the Old Testament, where Moses and the 70 elders were enveloped by the presence of God (Num. 11:25); in that presence, the anointing which was upon Moses was transferred to the 70 elders. In my own life, I was once in a church meeting where the minister was laying hands on people for powerful divine healings to take place; at the height of the service, the minister's eyes caught mine, and in an instant I felt a power emanating from him and into myself. For several weeks after that I experienced tremendous authority to lay hands on people and see them healed. Similar impartations commonly occur when people of great anointing minister under the manifesting presence of God.

The last example I gave you brings up the interesting point concerning how eyes may be paths through which spiritual energy flows. Proverbs 20:8 tells us how the ruler can disperse evil with the glance of his eyes. Similarly, a mother may bring her child under her reign with eye contact. John G. Lake, one of the most famous healing ministers of the twentieth century, used to explain how he liked to get eyeball-to-eyeball contact with a person from whom he was casting out a demon. Through such eye contact, authority may be exercised and power released.

Not only the eyes, but the hands are also *points of contact* for spiritual impartations and transferences. In the Old Testament times, the men of God often would lay their hands upon their children as they imparted specific blessings into their lives. This was a common practice in the early Church as well. Not only was the Holy Spirit imparted with the laying on of hands (e.g., Acts 8:17), but specific spiritual gifts were imparted also (e.g., I Tim 4:14). The practice of "laying on of hands" implies that spiritual substance actually flows through the hands of people. It is enlightening to read in the Bible of the time when Israel laid his hands upon the heads of his grandchildren, Manasseh and Ephraim. In that incident, a big issue was made concerning which child would have Israel's *right hand* upon him and which would have his left hand (Gen. 48:13-19). The point being made is that more authority flowed through Israel's right hand than through his left. The fact that differing points on the human body have *various values* in serving as *transmission points* brings many questions.

We have no intention of giving all of the answers here, but we can add that there also seem to be specific places on the human body which are more receptive to spiritual substances. For example, hands are laid upon the head to impart spiritual authority and blessings. Hands may be laid on an area of sickness to dispel that sickness from that location. Hands placed upon the shoulder of another person join the two in courage and faith. Feet may be blessed to add strength on a person's journey. The tongue may be touched to sanctify that which is spoken. Hands may be laid upon the temples of a person's head in order to help him/her change the visions in his/her mind. And hands may be placed upon the cheeks and upper neck to guard their emotions.

Of course, in pointing to these truths, we are not giving credence to inappropriate behavior related to "touch therapy" or practices involving immodest contact between people. We simply are noting how God made us, and that it is a fact that different points of our physical body are more sensitive to spiritual transmissions. The Apostle Paul warned Timothy not to lay hands on anyone too hastily (I Tim. 5:22). Spiritual impartations are real, and we must be wise in how we become involved.

It is worth mentioning a final, yet powerful condition for transmission. That is the sharing of what we sometimes call a "secret place." In this context, a *secret place* refers to the conditions in which a person places himself to find a complete state of rest. For example, a certain individual may have a place on a mountainside, in the forest, or by the sea where he goes to pray, to find peace, or to simply quiet himself. Others' secret places may be just in their own flowerbed behind their home. Or it may be sitting in front of a table with a cup of coffee when no one else is present. The secret place may not necessarily be a physical location, but rather a meditative condition in which an individual completely relaxes. It can be a place inside of oneself, where an individual turns his or her attention to block out the activities of the world and find complete solace. It also can be a memory that fixates one's attention because of its significance in establishing one's own life. A secret place is where a person anchors and finds himself.

When one individual allows another to go to a secret place with him, he is giving an invitation to touch his spirit. For this reason, a woman who desires the heart of a certain man may long to discover him in that state. Powerful bonding takes place when two people recall and discuss with each other the memories of past events which determined who they are and what they think in the present. A disciple may be changed radically the instant he experiences with his teacher such an open, unhindered condition. A hypnotist knows that if he can get his subject to relax to that state, he will have access to influence him with his spoken words. Once two people experience a secret place together, they have made a spiritual bond that links them and, hence, gives them ongoing access into each other's life.

People Functioning As a Unit

Spiritual dynamics influence who you are and how you act. Especially powerful are the expectations of the people around you. The more closely you are bonded to others, the greater will be the forces they exert upon your life.

Like planets in orbit within a solar system, so people are linked in relationships. Each planet moves and revolves in its own course, yet powerful gravitational forces act upon each one. In similar fashion, people have their own destinies and paths to walk, yet the spiritual dynamics occurring between us influence who we are, what we do, and what we think.

Especially powerful are the *initial impressions* people form of you. How you enter into a relationship determines to a large extent how people will continue to treat you in the future. If a person introduces himself to others as confident, and he continues to emanate confidence during the beginning of a relationship, others involved will expect that person always to be self-assured. Another individual who acts as a comedian in front of others will be expected to be funny in the future. For a similar reason, parents who nurture and care for their children will always tend to look at their offspring as "their children," regardless of their age.

These spiritual dynamics can be both positive and negative. On the positive side, it is comforting to know how you stand with friends and family. We can relax in the presence of people with whom we already know how to act. In addition, the expectations of others can add strength to our lives, so we continue to act as consistent, stable people.

On the negative side, the forces released by others' expectations can hold us in a type of prison. If we desire to change ourselves, it requires not only the energy to alter our own behavior, but also the inner strength to break, and then remold, the expectations of others.

The longer two or more people relate to each other, the greater will be the spiritual forces between them. These bonds can be so intense that their lives not only influence but actually depend upon each other.

In the Bible, we read of Jacob who so loved his son, Benjamin, that it was said, "... his life is bound up in the lad's life" (Gen. 44:30). In another passage, it is said that if Benjamin left his father, "... his father would die" (Gen. 44:22). We have observed similar dynamics in long-standing, close marriages where a spouse dies and a short time later the other also passes away.

Furthermore, two people may be bonded so closely that they feel the same hurts and pains. When one person is sick, the other also feels weak. A mother may be bonded tightly to her newborn infant, and when the baby has a restless night, the mother may experience immediate responses with every move of the child. An even more obvious proof of these spiritual bonds is the case where a grown child far away from the parents gets into trouble—perhaps a car wreck—and one or both of the parents will be disturbed within until they find out what happened. Many people have experienced such bonding with others, especially their own children and, as a consequence, been made aware of the hurts in that other person's life.

It is interesting to note how pain, burdens, or sorrow may be shared by people to the degree that it is lessened in the person who was first hurting. For example, when people visit a sick individual whom they love, they may leave feeling some discomfort within, but the sick person may feel a little better. Expressions of concern may do more than merely exchange words, but they may actually orient the hearts of people so that some measure of pain is relieved in the hurting person. There are also times when pain seems to be relieved in an individual through the touch of a loving person. *Can it be that spiritual*

45

substance is exchanged and strength is given to the sick person while some measure of pain may be transferred back to the healthy person? Yes, God has created us so we can share one another's burdens.

It is more than emotions, pain, sorrow, or intangible feelings that can be transmitted. Actual illnesses and physical disorders may be shared as well. For example, an individual may develop some form of cancer, and loved ones who visit that person may become more receptive to receiving similar forms of cancer. A mother may develop severe headaches which soon appear in one of her children.

Of course, such shared illnesses within family members could be accredited to genetic similarities, but evidence shows more than just that is possible. Real physical changes can happen among unrelated people who bond closely. For example, studies done on women in the military who live, work, and march together day after day reveal how their physical bodies may change to the extent that they all experience their menstrual cycles at the same time. People who have sympathy pains for another individual actually may develop the related illnesses. Yes, the physical body may change as bonding takes place or as spiritual substance is shared.

Among people closely bonded, we also see certain characteristics and habit patterns develop. For example, young boys in a street gang may talk and dress alike. Medical personnel who work closely with one another tend to share similar values and develop the same sense of humor. Even people who all attend the same church begin to laugh the same, dress alike, and view life from the same perspective. We are not implying that they become like "clones" of each other, but rather they develop "tendencies" toward similar behaviors and characteristics.

Not only do bonded people tend to think alike, but they may begin acting as if they share *a common mind*. One seems to know what the other is thinking. Amazingly, they may function as a unit, working together with very little verbal communication. It is as if they are all plugged into the same computer, aware of each other's needs and desires. Invisible lines of communication seem to exist between them, directing their actions and thoughts.

These group dynamics are real and can be observed in many situations of life, yet the concept of a common mind may seem a bit mystical for some readers. Since the Bible is our final authority on such subjects, let's look there for evidence.

When the Holy Spirit filled the early believers, we are told that they "... were of one heart and soul" (Acts 4:32). We understand that the Holy Spirit was enveloping and bathing them at that point. In that atmosphere they, indeed, did share a unity of thoughts and desires.

We also can read in the Old Testament concerning the Jewish people and how on several occasions they were molded together to act as "one man" (e.g., II Chron. 5:13, 30:12; Ezra 3:1).

Not only does the Bible declare that people can share a common mind, but we see this fact in many situations of life, especially where people must work together and depend upon each other. For example, individuals in war, police officers, firemen, paramedics, emergency workers, and others in life-threatening situations may learn to depend upon each other so intensely that when one needs the other, they automatically fill in the role. Similarly, in team sports the individual members may bond together so closely that they can work together and perform as if they are a unit. The even may not need to communicate with each other, but they simply "know" and move into the right positions at the right times.

One result of this common mind is a shared sense of responsibility. All the members of a team start working toward the same goal; however, they each do not carry out the same tasks. Instead, responsibilities seem to be distributed among them, so that they can work together, each fulfilling their individual role in the total purpose of the group.

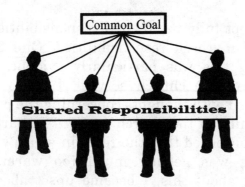

As any one person in a united group accepts responsibility for some area, it tends to decrease the sense of responsibility upon the others in that same area. Often, nothing needs to be communicated verbally. A spiritual dynamic is established wherein people united can act corporately and, hence, accomplish much more together than those working individually. We believe that God created mankind with this ability to work with others.

It is amazing to see how responsibilities can be shifted from one person to another in bonded relationships. A personal example I can give is from the time when I pastored a church. During the early years the church was small, and as the pastor, I had to oversee every area of the ministry, both practical and spiritual. Therefore, during the Sunday morning service I was thinking not only of the message to deliver, but also if the chairs were in place, the P.A. system was functioning correctly, the heat was adjusted appropriately, etc. After training several individuals to help with the ministry, I found that they could

49

not accept fully the related responsibilities until I gave up those responsibilities. One Sunday morning this was particularly evident. In the middle of the church service, I found myself consumed with thoughts concerning the practical functioning of the church service—in particular, I was concerned that the room in which we were meeting was getting much too warm. As I thought about this, I became upset about why one of my helpers was not aware of the problem and adjusting the heat. Rather than fix the problem myself or say anything, I decided to force myself to stop thinking about the heat. I knew I would be unable to bring forth an anointed message if I were consumed with thoughts about the physical comfort of the people. So I forcefully ejected any more thoughts concerning the heat. What I observed was that the instant I pushed the related concerns out of my mind, one of my helpers standing nearby me walked to the room thermostat and solved the problem.

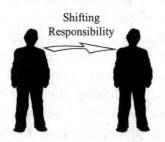

Shifting
Responsibility

The shifting of responsibility usually is not as simple as in the example I just gave. It typically requires much communication, training, and heart interaction. Also, shifting responsibility from one person to another usually entails a long-term process.

For example, in a well-functioning family the parents normally carry the sense of responsibility for the welfare of the children. If, however, the parents are unable or are negligent toward the care of their children, often one of the children, usually the oldest, will arise and carry many of the family responsibilities, to the best of his or her ability. In a marriage relationship, one person may be irresponsible financially, which leads the other to be overly responsible, perhaps even obsessed with money concerns.

What we see is that people exert spiritual pressure on others to whom they are bonded, as they accept or reject certain responsibilities. As people live under these spiritual pressures for an extended period, they may develop a lifestyle with the associated tendencies. A child forced to carry too much responsibility may pursue a career as an adult where great expectations are placed upon him, and he only may feel good about himself when such pressures continue to be placed upon him by others. On the other hand, a child who has received too much care (sheltered to an extreme) may grow up unable to deal with common stresses and trials, often leading to escape mechanisms such as alcoholism or drug abuse.

Because of these dynamics, a parent who worries too much about his/her children actually may be damaging them. The conscious or unconscious act of worry is often the acceptance of personal responsibility for the actions and welfare of another person to such an extent that person tends to become irresponsible. Such worry often is hidden in the life of a Christian parent behind prayers. Some parents may think that they are praying for their child, but actually they may be accepting so much responsibility for their child that they are "stealing the weight of responsibility" that should rest upon that child. Such "prayer" is destructive. The more they pray in this fashion, the more they may be releasing forces which make their own child irresponsible.

What we are instructed to do is to cast all of our cares upon the Lord (I Peter 5:7) or pray until the peace of God which surpasses all comprehension guards our hearts and minds (Phil. 4:6-7). Such a transference of a burden to the Lord actually creates a dynamic between God and the other person, where God can lay the weight of responsibility upon the appropriate individual. This is effective prayer.

Learning how to relinquish certain responsibilities to God, or just the yielding of responsibility to others, is key. A parent who carries too much may hinder his or her children. A businessman who constantly worries about his employees will keep his employees dependent upon him and unable to think for themselves. A pastor who wants to control every aspect of his church will hold his congregation in a state of immaturity.

Often the giving of responsibility to another person requires "dying to vision." To die in this sense means to abandon all efforts of fulfilling a certain vision that a person has within himself. This is often necessary because a vision-driven person may be so obsessed with his/her vision that no one else has "room" to help carry the load. Only if the vision is abandoned—that is the ownership is relinquished and shared with others—will those others actually help carry it.

Jesus explained:

> "Truly, truly, I say to you,
> unless a grain of wheat falls
> to the earth and dies, it re-
> mains by itself alone; but if
> it dies, it bears much fruit"
> (John 12:24).

Relate the grain of wheat in this parable to a God-inspired vision in a believer's heart. Jesus taught that unless the seed or the grain dies "it remains by itself alone." When a person is consumed with a vision, even a God-inspired vision, he will remain by himself alone—other people may help, but they must depend upon the constant energy input of the visionary. The visionary, indeed, may have enough energy to inspire everyone around, but immediately when that visionary is not around, the energy wanes in all who are involved. The visionary remains alone in carrying that vision.

However, if the seed dies, "it bears much fruit." When a visionary arrives at the point where his own hopes of ever accomplishing the desired goal—or even seeing it manifest—are dead, the energy to fulfill that vision will be planted in the hearts of those to whom he is bonded. To die, in this context, means to relax in the passion and zeal of that vision, even to relinquish the vision to such an extent that it is entrusted back to God and forgotten. When a person yields his own desires in this way, a vision may be planted in the hearts of those around.

Through such an impartation, visions may be shared and many people, hence, energized to carry out the related goals together. Often a visionary will be required to die to his own vision repeatedly before the spiritual energy is released or passed on to others. If it dies it, indeed, will "bear much fruit."

What we have learned is another way in which people can be made to act as a unit. Through all the means we have studied in this chapter, bonded individuals may come to a point of unity where they share a common mind, desires, and responsibilities. In addition, they can share a vision which unites them in deep ways so that they may function together as a unit.

In today's world, many psychologists have studied such group dynamics. They sometimes use the terminology *group consciousness*. What is interesting is that a person with a naturally based view of man's existence can observe, but can offer no explanation for these group interactions. The Bible-believing Christian, however, can. We understand that every person has a spirit/soul which exists in the spiritual world. That spirit/soul has the ability to bond with others. Spiritual energy is the light which illuminates men's minds, enabling them to think. The reason people seem to act as if they are united is because *they are united*. There is, indeed, a group consciousness among people who are bonded together.

The Human Spirit
And Authority

The next property of the human spirit which we need to discuss is how it both emanates and responds to authority.

Picture a group of people who all are seated in a classroom facing the front. If someone with great authority walks through the door at the back of the room, many of those seated will turn to see who walked into the room. On the other hand, if a person with very little spiritual presence walks in, almost no one will turn to see who entered the room. Such a phenomenon only can be explained by recognizing the fact that authority is something which can be sensed spiritually by others.

Not only can people sense authority, but their spirits actually yield to it—and, in a sense, bow to a person of greater authority. The Bible gives us an example of this when the Queen of Sheba met King Solomon. After the King showed her all his wealth, we are told in the Bible that "there was no more spirit in her" (I Kings 10:5).

The Queen was left speechless, awed by the blessings of God upon Solomon's life. Her spirit was left without strength in the presence of Solomon's grandeur.

We see that a similar reaction may occur in a person when he encounters God. For example, when the glory of God manifested in the temple, as recorded in the Old Testament, the priests were unable to stand. John fell as a dead man when Jesus appeared before him (Rev. 1:17). Isaiah had a similar experience, as recorded in Isaiah 6:1-5. All the soldiers that came to take Jesus from the Garden of Gethsemane fell back when Jesus declared who He was (John 18:6).

In some churches today, we see people being "slain in the spirit." There are, of course, false encounters of this phenomenon, but in true experiences, the person's spirit is bowing to the presence of God to such a degree that his/her body no longer has strength within it to continue standing.

Of course, "authority encounters" don't happen just in religious contexts, but frequently in our everyday lives. Today, an employee may be intimidated by his boss, which we understand is the result of his spirit yielding to that boss. For the same reason, a timid child may have to summon all his energy to talk to adults. Some people find themselves speechless in the presence of famous individuals. They cannot think as clearly, and their physical body actually can lose its strength as the spirit within is pulling back.

We do not want to put all forms of authority in the same category. Obviously, authority can be used either for God's glory or for evil purposes. We are not trying to make a distinction at this point, but are merely explaining how authority influences the human spirit. What we discover is that the human spirit is very responsive to the authority which abides in others.

Where, then, does authority originate? Romans 13:1 tells us, "...there is no authority except from God, and those which exist are established by God." God is the Source of all authority. When He spoke over Adam and Eve, "... fill the earth and subdue it," He instilled in the nature of mankind the authority to manage this world (Gen. 1:28). God has given each and every human being some measure of authority.

An individual's authority grows as he accepts the related responsibility. Jesus said, "For whoever has, to him shall more be given" (Mark 4:25a). Our Lord went on in the same Bible passage to say: "and whoever does not have, even what he has shall be taken away from him" (Mark 4:25b). As we apply this truth to authority, we can say that individuals will lose the authority upon their own lives if they do not embrace and use it.

The authority of a person also increases as they make deep heart decisions within themselves. For example, a young man may make a decision to escape the lifestyle of poverty in which he was raised and, hence, become a financial success. The strength of that decision, indeed, will increase his authority to accomplish his goals.

Many times the decisions that are made are negative and have negative effects upon the people around. For example, if a certain woman is deeply hurt in a relationship with a man, she consciously or unconsciously may make a firm decision never to expose her heart to another man again. As she makes that decision, she is exercising the authority she has over her own being, yet it will affect many other people throughout her life, and the depth of her decision will determine the strength of her authority in the related areas.

For another example, we can talk about a man who repeatedly has given himself to the abuse of alcohol. Because he has yielded to the temptation so many times, he may lose his own authority to control himself, while at the same time making deep decisions, such as, "I will do anything for another drink." That lifestyle will diminish his authority over his own self-discipline, yet it may give him authority to find his next drink.

Authority is especially increased as a person pays a high price for the decisions he has made. When other things are sacrificed or a person has had to stand against tremendous opposition, persecution, or trials, his heart commitment deepens. As a person's heart is pointed (*phroneated*) more and more firmly in a specific direction, it releases powerful spiritual forces which flow outward in the corresponding direction.

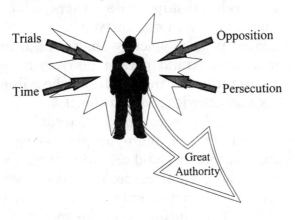

Similarly, authority grows as people invest more time and energy. People who have years of experience in a certain area develop more confidence in themselves and, hence, authority in their work.

Authority also can be obtained from another person. We saw this earlier as we discussed how Moses laid his hands upon Joshua and imparted some of his authority. In similar fashion, parents, teachers, or leaders can impart some of their authority to those under their care. As we mention the teacher/student relationship we are not saying that the authority of the teacher to govern the class may be passed on; instead, we are referring to how authority "in the related field of study" may be passed from teacher to student. Jesus said that a pupil will become like his teacher (Luke 6:40). A student who invests years at school may draw upon the strengths of his instructors. Similarly, an individual who develops close relationships with others who have authority may obtain authority.

Married people typically share authority. In fact, if a weak, timid person marries a person with great authority, in time he or she will begin to speak and act with more authority.

There is also a *corporate authority* which results from two or more people taking their individual authorities and orienting them toward the same goals. Their corporate authority is always greater than the sum of their individual authorities. This authority is the result of deep heart commitments.

The dynamic of *corporate authority* is so significant, we will discuss it in pages which follow, but we also will add to it what we have learned previously about group consciousness and shared responsibilities.

7

Corporate Authority In the Family

Once a group of people have become bonded together, they can fulfill a corporate function greater than can the individual elements. As we already explained, a corporate mind seems to develop, and people share responsibilities in an almost mystical sense. They, therefore, can work together and accomplish great tasks. Not only is work easier, but the authority upon them is greater. This authority flows out of the united group as if a spiritual stream were established in the spiritual realm. In this chapter, we will examine how this authority functions in the family unit.

First, consider a marriage. When a husband and wife join themselves together, they form a team to work united in this life. If they are in agreement, then together they have more authority than each does separately. This authority is very evident in the family atmosphere where children are raised. A husband and wife united in heart are able to create an environment where children can grow feeling secure and loved.

The spiritual influence which emanates from parents has a real effect upon the thoughts and decisions of their children. To some degree, it guides the decisions which the children will make throughout their lives.

Loving, Bonded Parents

Spiritual Flow

The authority stream from parents is *not forced* upon their children *nor automatically deposited* within the children's spirits. It is better to envision the stream as a "wind of influence" gently blowing over the thoughts, mind, and heart of each young one. The children must open or close their own hearts in order to receive or reject their parents' influence.

Consider now the case where parents separate through divorce. The family authority has been divided, and the spiritual influence, therefore, will be divided.

Let's say the husband, whom we will call John, has the young children visit him on weekends, and the mother, Carol, has the children stay with her on weekdays. While the children spend time with Carol, she will influence them according to her desires and beliefs. As long as the children's hearts are pointed toward their mother, she will be able to direct them easily.

Then, on weekends when the children visit their father, he takes over the spiritual headship. At first, John may find the children are moving in their daily lives contrary to his desires. But then after a day or two, their hearts will start pointing (*phroneating*) toward him, and he will have greater access to the influencing of their thoughts and actions.

Then, when it is time for the children to return to the care of their mother, Carol finds that the children seem to be going in a direction different than when she left them. She feels as if she must take the first two days just to get them back on track with her goals and plans. The pattern continues repeating itself, again and again. When the children's hearts are directed toward their mother, they respond to her, and then when they turn their hearts back to their father, they come under his influence.

What we see are two different authority lines, *like two streams,* flowing from the separated parents. The children submit to and draw upon the stream to which their hearts are pointed. Their thoughts and desires align with the father or mother, as they yield to the authority of each. When there is a divorce, there is not only the separation of two people, but also the division of a spiritual stream.

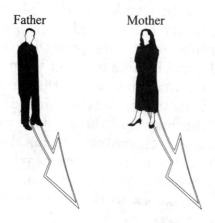

One Spiritual Stream Divided IntoTwo

Obviously, this paints a tragic picture for those who have experienced the related difficulties. We can reassure people at this point that God forgives, heals, and restores. We do not want to make the resulting problems seem hopeless. Later, we will talk about healing some of the wounds that may result from divided spiritual streams. Here, we just are laying the fundamentals of how authority works.

When a husband and wife realize they have the ability to form a spiritual stream for their descendants, they no longer limit their thinking to just themselves or their children. A marriage is, in fact, the merging of two streams in the earth. As two family lines are joined in marriage, a new entity is created. A stream of blessings and/or curses is released upon those who follow.

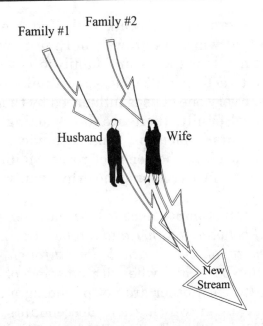

In our modern Western society, we tend not to think in these terms. People are much more focused upon present relationships than family lines. In Bible times, people thought much more "generationally." For this reason, family lineages are emphasized in the Scriptures, and it was important to know who was a descendant of whom. People today who do not think generationally are missing some profound truths.

Now as we explain this, we are not denying the freedom which we may find in Jesus Christ. We are taught in the Bible that Christians have been spiritually grafted into the family lineage of God. As such, we can escape, to some degree, the negative influences which may flow through our natural family lines.

As we grow in our walk with God, we may grow in that which we draw from Him. However, we must not deny the natural family forces which continue to act upon us. These spiritual streams are real. Every one of us is influenced by them. In our natural family, there are forces acting upon our thoughts, emotions, and behavior. This brings us back to the sense of responsibility we should have in developing healthy family relationships.

Of greatest importance is how the *strength of the bond between a father and mother determines the strength of the spiritual flow through their lives.* A husband and wife with no sense of commitment to each other are not providing a spiritual base upon which their descendants may stand. Those children will suffer for it. They more likely will be tossed by *other winds* throughout their lives, or they will tend to become a part of another group (sometimes a cult) which provides them with a spiritual base.

In contrast, a husband and wife deeply committed to one another establish strong forces in the spiritual realm in which their descendants can grow. Trials that come against that man and woman can be the means by which their authority increases. Sickness, lack of finances, personal struggles, etc., each demand that the husband and wife *phroneate* their hearts more wholly toward each other. That deepening commitment increases the spiritual flow through them. The longer they stay together and the more deeply they cling to each other, the greater will be their authority in the earth.

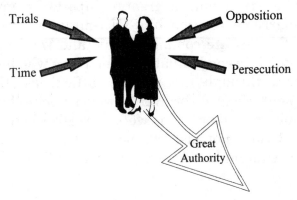

Trials — Opposition
Time — Persecution
Great Authority

That authority is not just for the present. We understand that the spiritual stream they create, through their covenant and bonding, transcends time. It goes wherever their hearts are pointed; if, therefore, they believe for their children, grandchildren, and beyond, then they will establish spiritual blessings in which the generations to follow will bathe.

On the other hand, when there are violations of the marriage covenant, there are also consequences which extend for years and years. Recall King David's sin when he committed adultery with Bathsheba (II Sam. 12:10-11). Even though David repented and God forgave him, God told David that his nation would suffer through inner turmoils and wars for many years to follow. Indeed, we see his sons deceptively fighting one another until the nation of Israel was divided. David once had been given authority over the nation; therefore, the entire nation was affected when his heart was divided.

This truth puts a greater importance upon the marriage relationship. Of course, we know that divorces are common today, and we do not want to place condemnation upon those who have suffered through the related difficulties. God does heal. He does forgive. However, seeing from the spiritual dimension, we can realize how divorce divides not just two people, but the spiritual stream intended to bathe a family line.

Authority Streams Throughout Society

The spiritual dynamics seen in family units, involving corporate authority, a common mind, and shared responsibilities, operate similarly in many other groups in which people work together.

Consider a local church. When there is a group of church elders committed to working together, they will develop an authority greater than will any single individual. The longer they work together, the greater will be their unity. Each time they face a problem, they will have to decide to continue working together or to separate and go their individual ways. As they stick it out and work through their differences, they are entering deeper and deeper into covenant relationships with each other. The more they invest in each other and in a common goal, the greater will be their corporate authority.

When we talk about this corporate authority in the Church, we also should mention *corporate anointing,* because the word *anointing* refers to the flow of the Holy Spirit. As Christians become of one heart and mind, the presence of God manifests. The Holy Spirit and the believers' spirits' become one. Therefore, the resulting authority has the added dimension of the flowing Holy Spirit.

Holy Spirit

Elders United in Heart

Corporate Anointing

The congregation benefits wondrously through this corporate anointing. The blessings of God flow. The people bathe in the love and sense of security produced. Their thoughts and desires melt together to some degree. As they yield to and enter the spiritual stream, they form into a united, loving body.

Consider, however, what will happen if there is a tragic split among the church leadership.

Let's say some of the elders go one way and the others go another. What will the people do? What will they experience?

Many congregational members will feel as though they have to choose between one set of elders or the other. When they visit with the first set of elders and listen to their side of the issues, they may begin to see things similarly. Then as they go visit the other elders, the average church member may switch his position to the opposing view. There even may not be any conversation related to the church split, but because spiritual streams are determined by heart-bonding, church members will start to think along the lines of the leaders their heart is pointed toward.

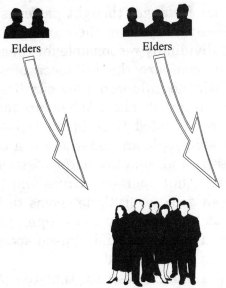

Elders   Elders

Congregation Tossed Back & Forth

Spiritual streams exist not only in churches or families, but all human beings have spiritual energy flowing out of them, and whenever people bond together, a corporate stream begins to be established. Strong streams are evident in businesses, big corporations, political associations, clubs, schools, football teams, musical groups, street gangs, etc. In every situation of life where people have commitments to each other, the spiritual energy from within them flows together. That spiritual energy can and does influence people's thoughts.

When we talk about these streams, we are not saying that people's thoughts are determined 100% by the outside spiritual influences acting upon them. Rather, we simply are pointing out streams that *influence* thought patterns. People still have authority over their own mind, and they are individually responsible for themselves.

We can compare the influence of spiritual streams with the influence a big city has upon a small community dweller. When an individual lives for an extended time in an isolated area with very few people around, there is a tendency to slow down and simplify one's lifestyle. However, when that person drives into a big metropolitan area, everything seems to be moving very quickly. In a very short time, that small community dweller will find himself speeding up to the pace of those around.

It is in a similar fashion, that the thoughts and beliefs of those around us exert pressure upon us. Not only those who are within a certain group are influenced, but outsiders who come against any spiritual stream also may be influenced.

These dynamics are very evident in an institution of higher learning. One mature, well-trained professor can exert tremendous pressure upon the thoughts of the young student. How much greater is the authority of the whole institution backed by hundreds of teachers, millions of dollars, and years of labor? A student just enrolling in such an institution should expect powerful forces to begin molding his or her thought patterns accordingly.

Similarly, we can look at a large mass of people united around a specific religious belief. If a person not strong in his own beliefs visits a Moslem country, where thousands of Moslems chant five times a day while facing Mecca, there will be a lasting impact upon his mind. His weak thought patterns even may "bow," and as a result, he no longer may remember what he used to believe or why.

From these examples, we can see the forces of spiritual streams reaching beyond small organizations or groups of people and actually flowing out to influence large regions of the world.

Such great forces are evident within every nation. As people work and play together, the corporate authority of a country develops. Any national activities, such as elections, the death of a leader, or even sports events, cause the people to orient their hearts in the same direction.

Perhaps the greatest forces are established for a nation as they go through a war together. In such conditions, the leaders must unite their people for their own defense. The resulting commitments among citizens can be extremely intense. Soldiers bond under life-and-death situations. Children and loved ones remaining at home may direct their hope, faith, and tears toward a common goal. Sacrifices are made, and some of the deepest bonds possible are formed with the yielding of blood. Such covenants produce spiritual forces. When thousands of people in one country all have their hearts *phroneated* down a common path, there are consequences in the spiritual realm. After a war is finished, the energy does not shut down quickly. Hate, fear, love, and passion are powerful forces orienting the hearts of people.

All such forces help to establish a nation's identity and cultural tendencies. The people to follow, therefore, will have similar thoughts for years to come.

The resulting spiritual streams transcend time. Remember that spiritual substance is not limited to the time restrictions which we know in the natural world. The spiritual breath which God breathed into Adam still is sustaining life generations later. So, also, spiritual substance released through human beings today may influence people who will live years down the road.

Changing or Escaping
A Spiritual Stream

People like to think that they are independent thinkers, free of the influence of others. That thought is a myth. We live in a world flooded with the thoughts and currents of other men and women—not just from those around us, but also from people who have gone on ahead of us, especially where corporate authority streams have been established. The Apostle Paul cautioned us not to be "tossed here and there by waves, and carried about by every wind of doctrine..." (Eph. 4:14). Even when we think we are being logical and every point we conclude logically follows the preceding one, we simply may be riding on the thought patterns established in the spiritual realm by others.

Realizing this raises questions concerning how then we can think freely today. Can we undo some of the negative consequences of our foreparents? Can we ever get a perspective from above the streams which tend to influence us? And is it possible to change the flow which goes beyond us to those who follow in our footsteps?

The answer is, "Yes," to all three questions.

First, we may undo the wrong decisions made by those preceding us. An example is when hate and bitterness have released forces which split a family in two, and later forgiveness heals and removes from the spiritual dimension the energy which stirred negative feelings.

To see an example of such a powerful undoing of evil, read in the Old Testament about the covenant which the Jews made with the Gibeonites. This covenant was not according to God's will. The Gibeonites disguised themselves one day and tricked the Jewish people into promising them that they would never hurt anyone of their people (Joshua 9). That covenant established forces in the spiritual dimension that influenced people for years afterward. It is in Second Samuel 21 that we can read how King Saul did not honor the covenant made by his forefathers, and this resulted in a famine in the nation of Israel. God held the Jews accountable to fulfill the covenants of their forefathers. When they did not, there were serious consequences. King David, however, sought the Lord to find out how he could end the resulting famine. God told David exactly what to do, and after he obeyed, the famine ended (II Sam. 21:1-14).

Another example of a man undoing the consequences of evil can be found in the Book of Daniel. At that time the Jewish people had been in captivity for their sins for 70 years. Daniel began fasting and praying for God to forgive their sins. He interceded, asking God to forgive the people; at times he prayed as if he were accepting personal responsibility for the sins of his foreparents (Dan. 9:1-19). God answered and, indeed, the Jews were set free.

Apply these principles to what happened through the Protestant Reformation. We can study Church history and learn of the great split in the Christian world during the 1500's. Most Christians will side with either the Protestant position or else with the Roman Catholic. It is not our point here to side with either, but to note the tremendous spiritual forces established at that point in history. Thousands of people died for their faith—on both sides. Roman Catholics and Protestants were killed by the thousands. Hate, fear, and faith directed the hearts of millions. The consequences of those forces are still in the earth today, influencing thoughts and directing men's lives.

Can we escape those forces or get a perspective from above those streams? Yes. We cannot list here everything necessary to end such influences, because God must guide individuals in unique steps of obedience. However, we can say that repentance for the sins of our forefathers is necessary, and that lifting ourselves above the spiritual influences is also a key.

Stepping above a certain spiritual stream usually requires a re-identification of oneself. For example, I do not like to consider myself a "Protestant" anymore, because the name *Protes-*

tant comes from the term, *Protesting One.* Personally, I am not protesting anything. That is not the core of my Christianity today. Abandoning a label such as that is, in part, a step to rise above the resulting spiritual forces.

See this principle in Paul's writings to the early believers. In First Corinthians, chapter three, Paul corrected the Christians for aligning their thoughts and allegiance to himself or to another leader named Apollos. He explained that when one group claimed to be "of Apollos," while others claimed to be "of Paul," they were thinking as immature babies. The lesson is that we should not limit ourselves to the influence of any one leader, but instead, we all should be "of Christ."

It is through such a position of maturity that we can rise above the spiritual influences acting upon us. When we place our allegiance in the One who sits on the throne of God, we lift ourselves higher in the spiritual dimension. To help us in this, we have an anchor which is the revealed Word of God and the truth of the living Holy Spirit. We cannot remove ourselves completely from the spiritual ocean around us, but we can do our best to keep our hearts in a current that glorifies God and exalts Jesus as Lord.

The last question we need to address along these lines is, "How can a person change the stream which flows through him to those who come after him?" It is not only ourselves who need to be freed. Our descendants and those who may follow in our footsteps should not be hindered by our errors. In fact, we want our influence to bless them.

It is possible to stop negative influences from being passed to one's descendants. Even if an individual has had to battle for years against the negative pressures from their forefathers, it is their personal resistance which stops the flow. A person is fighting for his/her children when he/she battles against temptation. Also, people need to make a decision in the depth of their own beings concerning the seriousness of the sins of their parents. If they have found an identity separate from their own forefathers, they can say with authority, "The curse stops here!"

Even more inspiring is how they may bring positive strength and new spiritual blessings into the authority line and pass it on to those who follow.

An example is Abraham receiving the blessings of God. When God spoke to Abraham, He promised to bless him and his descendants:

> "And I will make you a great nation,
> And I will bless you,
> And make your name great;
> And so you shall be a blessing...
> And in you all the families of the
>   earth shall be blessed" (Gen. 12:2-3).

As Abraham received this blessing, it not only came upon him, but also became available to his descendants.

This blessing was first passed on to Isaac, Abraham's son. Later Isaac had two sons and it is enlightening to see how the blessing was released into their lives. The first-born son was Esau and he was in line to receive the blessing. However, one day he traded his birthright to his brother, Jacob, for a single meal (Gen. 25:27-34; Heb. 12:16). The consequences affected not just the two brother's lives, but the blessing of God actually was transferred from Esau's line of descendants to Jacob's. Millions of people were removed from the blessing line, while others were brought into and under the blessings of God.

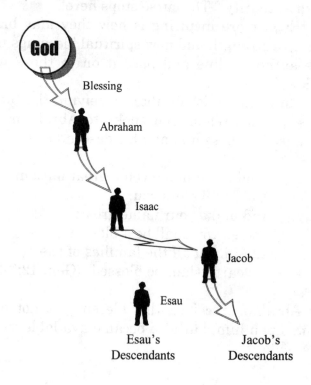

This transfer of spiritual blessing is another example of how spiritual impartations are not automatically deposited into certain individuals. Each person must accept or reject that which is offered to him or her. Once a spiritual stream has been established, it *makes available* to one's descendants the related benefits. However each person must choose whether or not to open their own hearts to receive.

Distinguish in your mind the difference between the words *importation* and *impartation*. *Importation* is used to identify the movement of new spiritual substance from out of the spiritual realm into a specific stream. *Impartation* is how that spiritual substance may move from one individual to others. An importation moved into the family line of Abraham through Abraham, while that blessing was imparted to his descendants through Isaac and then Jacob.

We can see more examples of this in the Bible. Hannah, for example, was a woman who cried out to God for a child, and in those prayers she agreed to dedicate that child to the Lord's service (I Sam. 1:9-19). As a result, she imported into her family line a specific blessing from God. That blessing was imparted to her child Samuel, who became a powerful and influential prophet of God.

We learn that parents actually can stand in the presence of God on behalf of those under their care. God, who sees in the realm of the spirit, is not limited to the present. When a person is standing in His presence, praying for some particular need, God sees not only the person, but also those to whom that individual is bonded. For example, a parent is bonded to his/her children, and God, Who sees in the spiritual dimension, can see those children linked with the parent. God tells us in the Bible that He will bless the person who loves Him and those blessings will extend to the generations after that individual (e.g., Ex. 20:5-6). Parents who understand this principle realize that they can stand in the presence of God and receive from God blessings—not only for themselves, but also for their offspring. Those blessings are not forced upon their descendants but do indeed become available to those willing to receive.

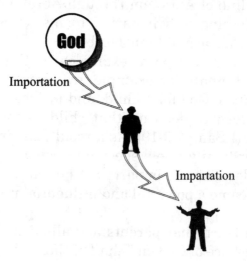

Evil also can be imported into a family stream, and then, imparted to those who follow.

The first example we have in the Bible is related to Adam's sin in the Garden of Eden. We are told that through Adam "...sin entered the world, and death through sin, and so death spread to all men..." (Rom 5:12). Notice how Adam was the doorway for death to enter into the world. That death then spreads to all descendants of Adam as they open themselves up to evil and sin.

We see this principle working in many ways in our daily lives. A father who yields himself to anger may import the related forces into his family line. As a consequence, his children may have strong forces released upon them pushing them to give in to similar anger problems.

Similarly, parents who repeatedly give in to sexual perversions may release like forces upon their own descendants.

Some would prefer to accredit such evil forces to social and psychological tendencies learned from parents. Of course, many behaviors are learned from those by whom we have been reared. However, we also want to identify the spiritual forces that can be released from parent to child.

These principles not only work in family relationships, but within all relationships where people are bonded together or sharing a spiritual stream. We have referred several times to the Scripture which tells us that when one part of the Body of Christ is blessed, we all are blessed; when one part hurts, we all hurt (I Cor. 12:26).

Negative spiritual substance can also be imported and transmitted through the united Body of Christ. Paul warned the Corinthian church about the sexually perverted man in their midst (I Cor. 5:1-8). The Apostle Paul explained that the evil influence flowing through this man could spread to the entire church. He rebuked the believers for allowing it in their presence:

> Do you not know that a little leaven leavens the whole lump of dough? (I Cor. 5:6b).

Notice the comparison Paul made with how yeast can spread and grow throughout an entire loaf of bread.

Spiritual "contamination" may flow not just down an authority or family line, but also outward to all who open their hearts up to the evil which is present.

It will be helpful to introduce one more term here, the word *porter*. We take this word from the service of a porter who assists us boarding a train or stands at the front door of a hotel or similar establishment assisting or forbidding certain people to enter. In similar fashion, any person can act as a porter, bringing in or restricting spiritual influences that would enter the stream of which they are a part.

Any and every human being acts as a porter to some degree. Within a single family unit, each person can import spiritual substance positively or negatively. A parent's anger may bring the entire household under emotional stress. A son may import a bad attitude, which he imparts to the others. On the positive side, one person may develop a strong positive attitude and great faith, by which everyone is lifted and strengthened. Or a parent may recognize a negative influence trying to enter the family and simply by an assertive stance refuse to allow its entrance.

Spiritual transmissions from one to another tend to flow from a person of authority to those with lesser authority. However, all people bonded together can and do influence each other to some degree. If the father of a certain family comes home one day with a bad attitude, he may unload on his wife, who takes it out on the children, who kick the dog. A strong child more easily can impart spiritual substance to the others than a timid child. People bonded together influence each other, but the strongest tendencies flow "downhill" in respect to authority.

Let's end this chapter with a positive example of the principles we have been learning. In a local church a certain leader may receive (import) some anointing, authority, or other blessing from God. All the people under the care of that leader eventually may benefit from what has been imported. They will not automatically receive the related blessings, however, as they open themselves up to receive they may indeed enter into the stream of blessing.

Spiritual Dynamics Between People

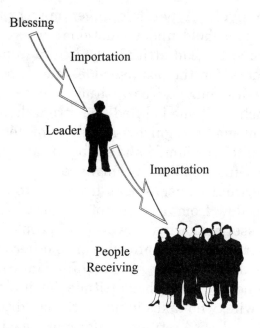

Blessing

Importation

Leader

Impartation

People
Receiving

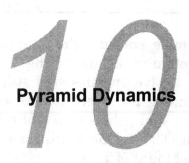

Pyramid Dynamics

We have explained much concerning where authority originates and how it affects people. Now, in order to teach key principles on authority dynamics, we want to use a geometric figure: the pyramid.

Before I discuss the pyramid and the authority principles revealed in it, I must defend my use of it. The reason is that many Christians wrongly have associated the pyramid symbol with evil spiritual practices. It is true that some occult practitioners use the pyramid in their evil works. Some who have negative views of the United States have seen the pyramid on the back of the American dollar bill and been warned that it is somehow associated with Satan's kingdom. Because of these misconceptions, I first must speak truth to you before I can explain what the symbol actually represents.

You should realize that the pyramid and the dynamics involved with the pyramid are used repeatedly in the Bible.

For example, consider the relationships commonly surrounding Jesus during His ministry. There were twelve apostles who stayed close by His side. Among the twelve there were three— Peter, James, and John—who had privileged access to Him. They alone saw Jesus revealed in glory on the Mount of Transfiguration, and later, weeping at the garden of Gethsemane. In addition to the twelve, there were seventy disciples who followed our Lord, and then there were crowds of 4,000 - 5,000 mentioned following Him at various times to hear His teaching. Of course, beyond these He blessed the multitudes and the entire world. If we arrange those numbers in a descending order of their commitment to Jesus, we have something like a pyramid.

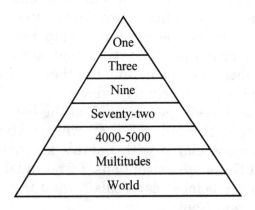

The same pattern of relationships assembled under the ministry of Moses. He had three close to him—Aaron, Miriam, and Joshua. Then he had the heads of the twelve tribes of Israel, and under those were the seventy elders. Below those in authority were the heads of the family units, and finally, the whole Jewish nation.

Our Lord taught several parables explaining how the Kingdom of God grows. He said it grows like seeds or leaven. Picture, then, how leaven, which is a yeast cell grows, and multiplies: first one, then two, then four, then eight, then sixteen, then thirty-two, etc. This type of growth, wherein numbers keep doubling, is exponential growth. Exponential growth in geometric form is represented by the pyramid. This is how our Lord said the Kingdom grows—thirty, sixty, a hundredfold (Mark 4:8)—first the blade, then the head, then the mature grain in the head (Mark 4:28).

Every living thing which God created grows in an exponential pattern. As plants yield their seeds, new growth begins. If reproduction is unhindered, they will go on reproducing generation after generation in the same proportions that a pyramid increases in size as we move to lower levels. Animals, too, if allowed to reproduce without death interfering, recreate the same pattern of growth. It permeates all of life.

It is also interesting to note the numbers that appear in the Book of Revelation concerning those who assemble around the throne of our Lord. We do not have the complete picture, but we are told about the twenty-four elders and the 144,000 who will carry out judgments in the earth. It is no coincidence that archeologists believe there are 144,000 stones in the perimeter of the bottom layer of the great pyramid in Egypt.

Now, I am not saying that the Egyptian pyramids are of God. Nor am I teaching that everything with a pyramid on it is good. Please do not assume that. Rather, I am trying to break the thinking which some Christians wrongly have embraced toward this symbol. Only then can I explain its significance, and why we see it repeatedly used in authority relationships in the Bible.

The pyramid symbolizes spiritual dynamics that occur in relationships involving authority. Of course, it can be used by evil men and women. In both the church and in the business world, there have been some organizations that have assembled under this structure in a fashion which allows leaders to control and manipulate those "under" them. We are not giving credence to such domination. However, the concept of cascading exponential growth—represented by the pyramid—is a truth which Christians should understand. This is how the Kingdom of God grows. It is in the Bible because it teaches us something.

When the pyramid is used in relationship to authority, it often is drawn with an eye positioned on the top portion of the pyramid. The great pyramid in Egypt has the top peak left off. On the back of the American dollar bill, the eye is positioned very prominently at the top.

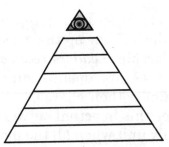

What is the significance of this symbol?

First, recognize that authority and blessings tend to "flow downhill." Those carrying authority are represented by the top portion of the pyramid, and those below are the people under the established authority. As we study relationships in real-life situations, we typically see these dynamics taking shape. Whether we are studying governments, corporations, organizations, businesses, schools, or families, there typically forms a structure of descending authority. These are the facts of life.

As we explained in an earlier chapter, authority is the result of people working together. Therefore, as we discuss pyramid dynamics, do not envision a cruel leader dominating a mass of people under his feet. On the contrary, every single person represented in the pyramid adds to the whole authority structure. The authority exercised by those in leadership is the result of all the people's hearts united together. As the people unite, they see the need to trust certain individuals with the oversight of what they hope to accomplish corporately. This is good. This is how God designed us to work together.

The eye, often pictured on top of the pyramid, symbolizes the effects of the people's trust on those in leadership. *Leaders receive the ability to lead.* Their eyes are opened supernaturally to guide those under their charge.

Please see this in actual outworking.

In a family unit when all the individual members of the family trust the father of that family, he will have more confidence to lead. As they trust their mother to fulfill her role, she will be guided supernaturally to fulfill that role. If one of the children falls into a dangerous situation, something within the father or mother may motivate them to go and check on that child. The incidents of such occurrences are common. The motivation a parent receives is not because they hear anything audibly, or see anything visibly, but one or the other is motivated instinctively— and spiritually—to go and correct the problem.

Similarly, in a business, when the president, boss, or others in charge are carrying the responsibility given to them, they will find themselves being supernaturally guided to fulfill their duties. If there is a financial difficulty, something inside the boss may nudge him to direct his attention to the problem. If there is a certain employee causing difficulties, the boss is likely to discover it. That discovery may be the result of his diligent oversight, or it may be just the result of a "coincidence" where he catches the problem out of the corner of his eye. Somehow everything under his charge will remain "open" to his oversight. The wise boss learns to trust his "gut feeling" in such cases.

This principle is given to us in many Scriptural references. For example, in the context of spiritual dynamics, John explained to us that the "...anointing teaches you..." (I John 2:27). Notice the supernatural guidance at work in the believer's life. The teaching to which the Scripture is referring here is not information received in school or out of a textbook. John went on to say that the anointing is "within you."

This is how all authority works. We are told in the Book of Romans 13:1 that every authority which exists has been established by God. God gives leaders wisdom to guide those under their charge—even non-Christian leaders.

The wisdom given not only is given by God, but it is the result of spiritual dynamics established among the people involved. As people trust their leaders, they literally are adding their individual authorities to him or her. A coach who has the hearts of his team will be a better coach. A father who is trusted by his family will be supernaturally guided to lead. A nation trusting in their king, president, or other government official is helping that leader to guide wisely. As a congregation looks to their pastor, his thoughts will clarify within his own mind, and he will be guided as to what to teach and say.

Let's apply these principles to leadership and the corporate setting of the Body of Christ. When a leader positions himself over the people of whom God has put him in charge, he will receive spiritual inspiration on how to lead. We are not talking here about a person asserting himself wrongly over others, but rather of a leader *accepting the responsibility* given to him by God. It is that accepting of responsibility which postures a person correctly over those whom he is to oversee.

Many pastors have learned how this works as they attempt to prepare teachings to bring to their congregation. If they do not know what to teach, they simply orient their hearts toward their people and accept responsibility for them. As they meditate on the needs of the people, spiritual energy flows through the pastor, enabling him to know how to help them. As the pastor positions himself between the authority of God and the draw of the people, the released flow of spiritual energy will inspire and direct his thoughts.

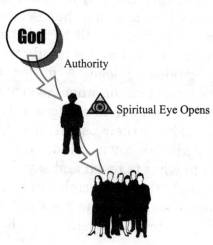

This is how all authority works. The businessman who meditates on his business will have thoughts aligning about how to run that business. The coach who accepts responsibility for his team will receive authority for that team—and the authority opens his eyes to see. A teacher who embraces his students as "his" students, and as "his" responsibility, will be motivated and inspired as to what to teach them.

Of course, some people may try to position themselves in places where they do not have authority (outside of their metron). If they do, they may open their minds to receive ideas concerning how to lead in the related areas, but those ideas have a tendency to be in error. For example, a sports fan who watches over a game may take the position wherein he sees himself as smarter than the coach; as he postures himself over the team, he soon will be having numerous ideas on how they could play better. His ideas, however, are not necessarily right, nor welcomed. Similarly, a Christian may judge a fellow Christian concerning how he is attempting to serve God. If he thinks it is his responsibility to judge, ideas will flow through his mind as to what his brother or sister is doing wrong. Those thoughts, however, may be carnal or even demonic in origin. In this fashion, when people assert themselves into positions of authority which are not theirs, they may open their discerning eyes, but what they discern has a tendency to be wrong

This last truth will become more evident as we discuss relationship violations in the next chapter.

11

Authority, Covenant & Free Will Violations

In explaining key spiritual dynamics, we have opened certain doors not only for understanding, but also for possible abuse. Some people may read the things we have taught and see in them opportunities to manipulate others or to gain self-serving authority. To the contrary, we are attempting to understand when it is right and when it is wrong to use spiritual authority. Therefore, let's discuss violations which may take place in relationship to authority, covenants, and free will.

Violations of Authority

We explained how a leader's eye opens when others submit to, believe in, and trust in him. This applies not only to group interaction, but also in one-on-one relationships. In the case where a person comes to a counselor for help and guidance, the counselee's trusting heart adds to the authority of the counselor. In the presence of the trusting individual, the counselor will have thoughts arise within that help give needed answers. It is not only education, experience, or previous training which provides answers, but the faith of the counselee draws upon the spiritual energy within the counselor to inspire thoughts and give direction.

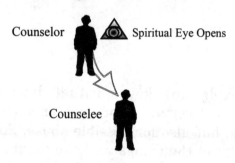

Counselor   Spiritual Eye Opens

Counselee

This dynamic also can be used wrongly. For example, people involved in mind reading take advantage of this. There are many who claim to have mind-reading abilities, but it is merely a hoax. However, there are some who can determine the thoughts of others through triggering the very dynamics which we have been describing.

As we explain this, do not think of mind reading as some strange, mysterious gift, because most people experience this "gift" to some degree. For example, two people who have been married for a long time often can "finish each other's sentences" as they communicate with each other. This is due in part to their familiarity with each other, but it is also a result of the common mind they share through their spiritual bond.

With mind readers, there is temporary spiritual connection made with their subjects. It is common for mind readers to posture themselves in an authoritative—even domineering—role over their subject, to such an extent that their subject is intimidated. Usually a mystical air is created around the mind reader. The person coming in for a mind reading exercise is placed in a submissive, even worshipful posture. In the place of awe before the mind reader, the subject may pull on the mind reader's spirit to inspire the very thoughts which they are thinking. The mind reader does not struggle to know what the person is thinking, but simply extends his spirit above his subject and allows the intimidating environment to cause thoughts to arise from within. These thoughts to some degree will be similar to the thoughts of the subject.

This, of course, is evil. It is a violation of people's individual authority. To see this, picture God-given authority as a light ray flowing from God to each individual. God has given each human being authority to manage his own life and to make his own decisions. An individual may go to another person, willingly submit to him, and receive his input; however, the individual maintains his free will in this. When a mind reader attempts to read another person's thoughts, he projects his spirit above that individual in a domineering position, placing himself between another human being and God. It is a violation or intrusion into the life of another.

Furthermore, when authority is being violated, the door is open to demonic activities. When people use spiritual powers not in God's will, they remove themselves from the realm of His blessings and expose themselves to the evil side. This is evident in the activities of mind readers, as devils may take advantage of the conditions and become involved, further inspiring thoughts and giving information to control and manipulate individuals.

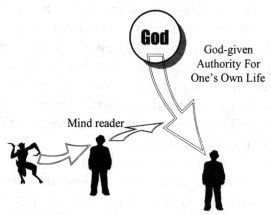

God

God-given
Authority For
One's Own Life

Mind reader

The mind reader is different from the counselor in that no mystical, deceiving air is required by the counselor. Furthermore, the counselee willingly is looking to the counselor for direction, fully aware of his own responsibility over his own mind. The mind reader violates the God-given authority of the individual.

A similar violation can be seen in the New Testament when Jesus warned the disciples about the religious leaders of the day:

"The scribes and the Phar-
isees have seated them-
selves in the chair of Moses;
therefore all that they tell
you, do and observe, but do
not do according to their
deeds; for they say things,
and do not do them...they
love the place of honor at
banquets and the chief seats
in the synagogues, and re-
spectful greetings in the
market places, and being
called by men, 'Rabbi'"
(Matt. 23:2-7).

The religious leaders had "seated themselves"—
that is, they claimed for themselves—the seat of
Moses, which is the position to lead the whole
Jewish nation. Notice that in that position of
authority they had true things to say, and Jesus
instructed the disciples to obey their words. However, the religious leaders had *put themselves* in
those positions, which is a violation of God-given
authority.

That is the whole issue: to use the authority
which God gives and not to go beyond it. In
Volume 4, we introduced the term *metron* which
is the Greek word usually interpreted in the New
Testament as *measure*. An individual's metron is
the measure of his God-given authority or *the
sphere of his influence*. The Apostle Paul, in

writing to the Corinthians, said he would not go beyond his metron, and, in particular, not exercise authority over peoples whom God had not given to him. However, he did speak with authority to the Corinthian people over whom he had labored in the past and who, therefore, were within his God-given authority (II Cor. 10:8-16).

The truth of this is key. When people exalt themselves into a position which God has not given them, they are stepping out of God's will, may be deceived in what they discern, and may be releasing evil spiritual forces.

An excellent example of this is the activities of psychics. Of course, there are some who claim to have the ability to mysteriously provide information about other people's lives and to predict their future; however, they are deceivers, simply saying things that easily are believed and twisted by the naive listener. However, there are also real psychics who can exercise such powers (e.g., Acts 16:16). We are not giving credence to them; in fact, the Bible clearly warns us that all such activity is abominable in the sight of God (Deut. 18:10-12). What we are doing is recognizing the existence of such evil people and how they, indeed, deceive others.

Being Christians endeavoring to understand spiritual dynamics, we can see how the trust and submissive attitude of a foolish person contacting a psychic, indeed, could open the spiritual sensitivity of the psychic. When a person sits in the presence of a medium or spiritist, his wrongly placed faith may open spiritual eyes to see. Or when a person contacts some of those who offer psychic services via telephone, the psychic, indeed, may be tapped into some demonic influence. Either way, they are stepping beyond God-given authority and, therefore, opening the door for evil spiritual influences.

Sometimes Christians worry that the present-day use of prophecy in some churches is just another form of psychic activity. There is a fundamental difference, however. In the church environment, we have people whose eyes are focused upon God and glorifying our Lord Jesus. Yes, prophecy is a spiritual activity, but the orientation of one's heart determines which spirit will be accessed.

Also, we expect proper authority lines to be respected within a church that exercises gifts of prophecy.

We should be concerned when the prophecy in our churches is being used by an individual who is stepping beyond his God-given authority. For example, if a young Christian walks into a certain local church and begins to prophesy negative things about that congregation or the church leadership, he is stepping beyond his metron. It would be impossible for him to receive such information without first "posturing himself spiritually over the church." However, that is not his God-given position. He, indeed, may receive some true information while he usurps that role; however, he will also be deceived to some degree in what he receives.

Repeatedly, I have seen these dynamics working in my own life. For several years I have been traveling and ministering in churches in many nations around the world. I am known, in part, for the gift of prophecy on my life. I have observed that when the leaders of individual churches look to me to speak direction to their particular situation, God does open my eyes to see and loosens my tongue to speak very accurately. However, early in the traveling ministry, I often offered my "spiritual insight" *without* the leaders' openness or willingness to receive. I was speaking from a sincere heart and thought I was doing God's will. However, as I look back over the thousands of people over whom I have prophesied, I have learned that my accuracy very much depended upon the people giving me authority in their lives. In the past, when I exalted myself and took a place above the people, at times I received accurate information, but I also saw how I made some serious mistakes.

Our eye is open to that which is beneath us. Again, let me say that when we exalt ourselves to a higher position, our eye is not as accurate, and we even may release evil spiritual influences.

Another example concerns the welfare of a nation. I have heard numerous well-meaning Christians prophesy about some catastrophic event—such as a major earthquake or flood—coming upon a people in judgment. I rarely put any value on such prophecies unless the person speaking already has from God the corresponding authority.

This has some profound implications. For example, if a president or king of a country saw a vision of an earthquake coming upon his nation, I would put more value on that vision than I would if a sincere, young Christian saw a similar vision. This holds true even if that president or king is a non-Christian. What enables a person to perceive things accurately is not whether or not, they are a Christian, but whether they have God-given authority. For evidence of this, we can see several examples in the Bible where kings—even ungodly ones—received visions of the future pertaining to their nation and those visions came to. pass. On the other hand, I have seen many well-meaning Christians prophesy things that never did come true because they were prophesying beyond their metron.

Of course, there may be times when a Christian receives something pertaining to the world beyond his present authority, but it simply will be a glimpse, and I do not trust such glimpses unless they are confirmed by the mouth of two or three others with prophetic giftings (I Cor. 14:29). *It requires a corporate anointing to accurately perceive things greater than an individual's authority.*

Violations of Covenants

Another area of concern worth mentioning here is how some people, including Christians, may bond with individuals outside their established covenants deeper than they do with those with whom they have already covenanted. Such bonding leads to a form of *spiritual adultery*.

For example, if a team of intercessors spend much time going into the presence of God together, they inevitably will bond one to another. Sometimes, however, the intercessors will be individuals separated in heart from their marriage partners. Perhaps their mates are not so interested in spiritual things, or they are simply not involved at that particular time. Because the intercessors are bonding deeply, they actually may become closer to each other than they are to their spouses. This is a violation of the marriage covenant, because God has so ordained that two are to become one in marriage.

What happens is that those involved soon are unable to communicate very well with their spouses. They feel drawn increasingly to be more and more with the new group to whom they are bonded, and their own families begin to feel distant or even estranged from them.

There are some cases when such bonding is allowed, such as for a short period during which intercessors are "praying through" something specific. However, long-term bonding which damages family relationships rarely is blessed by God. Repeatedly, I have seen God's intervention in such bonding relationships. Often those involved have what I call a "Tower of Babel Experience." They may be coming into great unity with each other and even accomplishing significant feats spiritually. But because they are allowing the covenants they have with their spouses and children to be violated, God intervenes. Usually, they think it is the devil attacking them and, indeed, God may be allowing the devil to have access to the situation. However, it is God actually saving them from more long-term personal destruction.

Violations of Free Will

Another caution I should mention here is that of violating another person's will through spiritual activities. The most obvious example of this is the practice of hypnotism. There are some hypnotists who take control of their subjects to such an extent that they no longer are able to exercise their free will.

How does hypnotism work? A hypnotist must take his subject into the spiritual dimension, form a bond, and bring him into harmony. Rhythmic motion, such as a swinging pendulum, may be used. Soothing music or a mystifying tone in the hypnotist's voice may be employed. The hypnotist must be trusted by the subject to such an extent that the subject will relax into an altered state of consciousness, wherein the hypnotist has free access to speak into the spirit of the subject.

Some people claiming to have hypnotic power actually are using only the power of manipulation, which is entirely different. For example, if a hypnotist performs on television in front of an audience, he may captivate the hearts and attention of all the observers, and then get them to focus on the volunteer subject seated in the front. Under such conditions, there are tremendous forces at work to make the subject do what the person claiming hypnotic powers asks. If the subject merely is yielding to suggestions because he wants to and/or because thousands of people are watching, then a force of manipulation is being used, rather than a power of hypnotism. The two may seem alike to the onlooker, but they are very different.

True hypnotism places the subject in a relaxed, trusting, open state of mind to such a degree that the hypnotist can speak directly into the spirit of the individual. In that condition, the person is unable to resist that which is said or asked. The forces of an observing audience are not needed. The authority of the hypnotist is exerted over the individual so that the subject will do whatever he is commanded.

In true hypnotism, the subject's free will is violated. Because of this, we must question at what point demonic activity becomes involved. We are not saying that all hypnotism involves demonic activity. That would be wrong to say. However, when one person violates the free will of another person, the door is open to demonic activity. It is the open door of which we must be aware.

There are also other spiritual dynamics at work in the hypnotic state. For example, the hypnotist and the subject will have a bond formed in the spirit, and that bond unites the spirit of one to the spirit of the other. This bond may be short-term or it may have lasting effects, even years later. Because of this bond, there will be spiritual exchanges occurring, especially as the hypnotist speaks words into the spirit of the subject. A person who puts himself into such a submissive state may have his own thoughts and beliefs altered for the rest of his life (unless God intervenes to heal). Often, words do not even have to be spoken. Because the spiritual connection has been made, that which flows from the hypnotist can change the behavior and belief system of the subject.

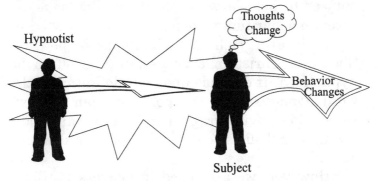

For this reason, we cannot believe always what a subject says while under the influence of a hypnotist. The subject, in fact, will often say what the hypnotist believes or wants the subject to say. For example, if the hypnotist believes the subject was sexually abused years earlier, the subject may say he was sexually abused, whether or not this was true. The thought and the belief

111

comes from the hypnotist and flows through the mind of the subject. Likewise, a hypnotist who believes his subject was taken up by aliens to another planet, without ever saying anything about this topic, will implant the related thoughts in the subject's mind. A subject can leave such an experience and honestly believe from that day forward that the events, indeed, did happen.

Now, we are not denying all hypnotic reports of sexual abuse, nor are we trying to explain here all the reports of alien abduction. Here we simply are showing how the relationship established between a subject and a hypnotist causes the subject to believe what the hypnotist believes, through a spiritual transfer.

Is it ever right to use hypnotic powers? Should a Christian ever permit himself to be hypnotized? It depends upon our definition of the word *hypnotism*. In the non-Christian context, we are identifying tragic results that can occur: changes in beliefs and open doors for demonic activity.

However, we also need to address the hypnotic conditions which sometimes take place within the Christian environment. For example, when a sincere believer comes forward to receive prayer at an altar call after an intense church service, all the conditions necessary for a hypnotic state may be at work. Similarly, certain counseling situations, such as those involving inner healing or intense exposure of one's past, activate real hypnotic forces. Even when believers pray together for an extended period, they may go into the exact same state of consciousness as do those who are hypnotized. Are we to deny these experiences or reject them as evil? No. There even are times when a certain minister will speak into the life of a submissive, yielded individual, and those words will change the course of that individual's entire life. Is this wrong? No.

Spirit-to-spirit contact is not wrong, but it is life-changing and powerful. We are not condemning it, but rather warning people about the dangers. When people step beyond their metrons, they open the door for demonic activity. When they yield themselves spiritually to another person, they may receive spiritual substance from that person which changes their thought patterns for years down the road. However, it is also true that some of us need a transformation of our thoughts, and to have someone speak spirit-to-spirit would help us tremendously in our individual lives. This is not something with which to play, but it is possible to be used for the glory of God.

We also must consider the use of hypnotism in the context of a person trying to overcome a certain bad habit, such as smoking. Or we can ask if it is right to use hypnotism to relieve physical pain, as is done sometimes. Or should people use self-hypnotism, listening to soothing tapes while they are relaxed in order to reprogram their subconscious?

As Christians, we cannot condemn such practices outrightly. Spirit-to-spirit communication which does change a person's subconscious thinking patterns is not necessarily evil. However, we approach this whole subject with caution, realizing the dangers that may be involved. Compare it with a medical doctor preparing to perform surgery on you. You would not want him putting you under anesthesia, cutting you open, taking out certain parts, and then putting other things inside you unless you had complete confidence in him. How much more cautious you should be in allowing another person to enter your spirit and remove certain beliefs, thoughts, memories, or feelings. Unless you know that nothing negative or evil is going to be placed within, you never should allow anyone that kind of authority over your will.

Finally, concerning hypnotism, we should say that if it is necessary for a certain Christian to undergo hypnotism, any and all sessions should be monitored by another Christian who is trusted and who will prevent any violations of free will or replacement of Christian beliefs.

Spirit Fixations

The seriousness of the above violations can be seen as we note the consequences which can last a lifetime. In an earlier chapter, we explained how the expectations of others release pressures upon us to be and act in certain ways. As planets moving within one solar system, the hearts of people exert invisible forces upon each other. Because of these spiritual dynamics, the violations which we have discussed in this chapter affect not just one person, but many—and often for years.

For example, consider Homer who was sexually abused by his Uncle Orville. When Homer was only eight years old, his uncle overpowered him physically, mentally, and emotionally. It left scars upon his life. His spirit/soul even may have taken on a subjugated, victimized posture. Homer may take on that posture with all other people in the future, or he simply may slip into that victimized posture in the presence of other people who remind him of his Uncle Orville. In either case, the stamp or impression left upon Homer's spirit/soul may last for his entire life.

What we see are *spirit fixations*, referring to how the human spirit/soul can take on a specific, unchanging posture toward others, circumstances, or events. We would include under spirit fixations the lasting effects induced by hypnotists, and any violations of a person's free will which hinders his ability to govern his own life in the future. Sometimes the bonding between two people can be so intense that it incapacitates one or the other person from ever thinking or acting independently. Also, violations of authority, where one person dominates another, may leave the subjugated person paralyzed in normal-life decisions.

These symptoms can be seen on an individual level, within a family unit, in an organization, or even throughout an entire society. For example, in countries where strong communistic control was exercised over people for many years, those who eventually come out from under that form of government often continue to live in fear, with an inability to advance as individuals. We understand that the spiritual energy within them has been quenched or suppressed to the extent that it does not flow out strongly enough to allow much creative thought, personal motivation, or forces to further personal goals.

It is not only the spiritual energy within a person which becomes established, but also the ongoing relationships with other people may fix spiritual forces which govern the future. This is especially true when two people have a deep, bonded relationship. What they believe about each other establishes forces which hold the other person in his or her present role. It is, therefore, more difficult to change. What we see is that spirit fixations may happen not only to individuals, but also to people bonded together as a whole. All such fixations can be difficult to break. Hence, the behavior of the people involved may be difficult to change.

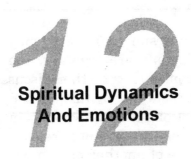

Spiritual Dynamics
And Emotions

Throughout these writings, we have attempted to see man as a whole person. What occurs in the spirit influences the soul and body. What happens to the body influences the spirit and soul. The entire man is engaged as three gears; when one moves, so also do the others. In similar fashion, whatever occurs in one part of man's being influences the other parts.

We have talked much about how the thoughts of a person are influenced by the spiritual dynamics occurring around them. In this final chapter, let's see how intertwined our emotions are with the spiritual dynamics occurring between people. Emotions have certain biochemical changes associated with them in the physical body. So, also, there are spiritual dynamics occurring with every emotion experienced.

For example, the sensation which is felt commonly as two people fall in love is the result of life-energies being exchanged between the two. As a boy and a girl catch each other's eyes, a transmission of spiritual energy may be felt. The longer two people are together, the deeper the bonding becomes (For further discussion of this, read *Two Become One* by this author.)

The emotions associated with mourning are just the opposite. A person is releasing the spiritual substance of another person who was loved. If an individual is dying of some illness in a hospital, the living family members may hold on for a time, keeping their hope and love directed toward the sick person. Their hope and love actually will extend spiritual strength to that sick person. If, however, the person dies, they in time will let go and experience a period of mourning. Mourning is the posturing of one's soul to release the spiritual energy of another person.

Loneliness is associated with weakening of another person's spiritual presence. When a person cries as a loved one is leaving, he/she is feeling the spiritual sensation of a bond diminishing in strength.

Anger usually involves the commanding of one's own spiritual energy to *phroneate*, that is, to focus and be directed in one place. For example, when an individual is angry at another person, he/she may direct all his/her passions and thoughts toward him/her. Similarly, anger may be directed at circumstances, events or things, and, hence, one's spiritual energy is turned forcefully upon those things involved.

In some situations, anger reorients the heart so that it is torn away from a person previously loved and/or admired. It is interesting to note how a dramatic shift in thinking may accompany such re-orientations of heart. This can be compared with two magnets which were once attracted to each other, but the polarity of one was reversed so that now the two magnets repel each other. Similarly, two people, while they are bonded, will share many similar thought patterns and desires. However, if they *phroneate* their hearts against each other, the change in the flow of spiritual energy between them may dramatically alter their thoughts and desires. They even may begin holding exactly opposite positions on certain key issues in their lives. Or one may begin despising whatever the other person loves. We can explain this phenomenon as we understand how the flow of spiritual energy influences our entire beings, and polarized spiritual energy tends to form opposing views and desires.

Because of this dynamic, any person who is *phroneated* against a certain other person, organization, or group of people to whom he or she previously was bonded, will have thought patterns and views which are distorted in the opposing direction. This is perhaps most obvious when a married couple are having a quarrel, and the two immediately see things in exaggerated opposing views. It is not until their emotions calm and their hearts are no longer antagonistic that reality and actual facts can be known. Similarly, when an individual angrily pulls away from a certain group (even a church) to which he was bonded previously, for a time he is likely to experience thought patterns and desires exaggerated in the extreme opposite positions. We each like to think that we are logical and correct in our views, but it is a fact that every person is subject to these spiritual dynamics.

We even can note that many bizarre or strange beliefs, political stands, social ideas, and religious doctrines are the result of people angrily ripping their hearts from others whom they previously loved and/or trusted.

Another emotion associated with spiritual dynamics is jealousy. Typically, this is the result of seeing a loved person point his/her heart toward a third person. For example, when a wife sees her husband admire a pretty girl walking by, she may feel her husband's heart chasing after that outsider. She may be aware that his heart is *phroneating* away from her and, hence, spiritual energy is turning. That can give rise to jealousy within one.

Now, we are not giving approval to all of these emotions and their related expressions. We simply are explaining how some of them may be stirred within people through spiritual dynamics. There is a time when jealousy is right and a time when it is wrong. God Himself declared that He is a jealous God, demanding that our hearts not turn toward idols (Ex. 20:3-5). Anger, too, is an emotion that can be used rightly or wrongly. Ephesians 4:26 tells us: "...be angry, and yet do not sin...." Emotions are created as a part of our nature. We are not trying to discern good expressions from bad ones here. Rather, we just are showing how closely they may be tied to the spiritual dynamics occurring between people.

Some of the greatest pleasures of life result from dynamics between people's spirits. Laughter is best when shared with another person who also is letting down the walls of his/her heart. When two people share some experience, such as looking at a beautiful sunset, they also may feel the energy exchanged between them. Because of this dynamic, it is natural for a person to want to share good experiences with a loved one.

Perhaps the most difficult emotional struggles are associated with the breaking of spiritual bonds. We already have mentioned mourning, loneliness, and anger, but it is also true that sometimes people will choose to end certain relationships by taking an assertive posture of spirit/soul. In doing so, a person may experience feelings of anger, mourning, loneliness, etc. In order to finalize the breaking of certain strong relationships, a person may have to harden themselves, that is, deny the feelings associated with the weakening relationships.

It usually takes an even more assertive, authoritative stance to disrupt the spiritual forces which others put on an individual through their expectations. As we explained previously, people release strong spiritual forces by the thoughts and views they have of others. Therefore, if a certain person is going to try to making significant changes in his life, he will be required to forcefully reject the pressures applied by others, and even change their expectations of him.

This is not to say that the forces released by other people are all bad. No. We were designed by God to need anchor points for our spirit. A healthy person is tied to a spouse, parents, friends, a larger group (including the Church), and God. Everyone of these relationships establish who we are, influencing our thoughts, behavior, and emotions.

When any of our relationships are broken, a *sensation of wandering* may be experienced. This is easy to understand as we realize that the ties are real spiritual bonds, and our being may be searching for new places to anchor.

Immediately after long-standing bonds are broken, there may be a tendency in a person to seek out new places to attach. A person recently divorced may grasp for a new relationship. An individual who has moved away from family and friends may start new relationships with the first people he or she meets. A child who has been rebuked harshly by his parents quickly may reach out to nearby friends for companionship.

Times following broken relationships are also times when people seek more earnestly for God and spiritual experiences. Studies show that people are more likely to make religious commitments during crisis times of their lives. This is not to diminish the significance of those commitments, but to recognize the spiritual voids which may lead a person to find fulfillment in God.

Voids in people's spirits also can cause them to create a situation in which others will be forced to orient their hearts toward them. For example, some people tend to create a crisis whenever they are lacking the love they need. They may have a car accident, a financial disaster, or some other problem which will gain for them the attention they need. Other people may misbehave, as a child who throws a temper tantrum or a teenager who rebels. Because the need for others' spiritual energy is essential for life, people consciously or subconsciously do whatever is necessary in order to obtain it.

Another emotion stirred spiritually is that of having one's hopes crushed. Proverbs 13:12 tells us that "hope deferred makes the heart sick." We can understand this as we see how hope entails the orientation of one's heart toward a desired goal. As some circumstances arise which make the fulfillment of that desire unreachable or delayed for a long period, then the spiritual energy which previously was emanating may wane. Since the heart is the fountainhead of our spiritual flow, it feels that sensation and suffers.

With similar dynamics, the turning of a person's heart from one goal to another may cause an emotion of sadness. This is especially true for people who are very focused in their lives, who tend to direct all their desires, thoughts, and spiritual energies in one place at a time. When they are required to re-orient themselves, they may go through a sensation of mourning, confusion, and hopelessness. They may feel as if they are "dying" as the spiritual energy within them is detached from one area and then seeks to anchor anew.

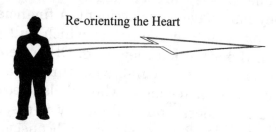

Re-orienting the Heart

All of us experience such sensations in our daily lives; however, we rarely see the spiritual dynamics taking place at the foundation of these emotions. Recognizing the link between our invisible side and our natural side, we also could talk about the biochemical and physiological changes that take place as emotions are stirred. What we see is that spiritual dynamics are completely *engaged* with physical dynamics. This is how God created us.

A final example of this correlation can be seen as we consider how a person may be thrilled for a brief moment, and others see a "gleam in his/her eye." That gleam at times may be spiritual energy piercing outward for a brief instant. The eye is the window of the soul, or as Jesus told us, it is the lamp to the body (Matt. 6:22). Of course, we could accredit such a gleam to natural processes triggered by a rush of adrenaline through a person's bloodstream, and all of the related physical changes, but we hope you see how both physical and spiritual changes may occur simultaneously.

Such is man's existence. Where there is physical change, there is spiritual change—and vice versa.

Conclusion

Every human being, whether or not he realizes it, experiences and lives with the spiritual dynamics which we have been discussing. Even people who think only in terms of natural forces have a spirit which sustains their life and allows them to think and interact with those around them. All of us were created with a spirit and that spirit is influenced by unseen forces 24 hours of each day.

These are facts of life.

Because we live in a world of interacting spiritual forces, we can point out the peace and order which results from a life in harmony with God and our neighbors. When a person finds peace with God and *phroneates* his heart toward Him, the force of God's blessings will flow through him. As people keep the covenants which they have established with other people, such as honoring their marriage vows, paying their bills, forgiving those who offend them, obeying the laws of their land, doing good to others, etc., spiritual authority will establish peace around them. On the other hand, when individuals violate established authorities or covenants, they cause turbulence in the spiritual dimension that disrupts people like a wave ever expanding upon a pond into which a rock has been tossed. In this light, we also see the promises of God in operation: when people seek first the Kingdom of God, forces are released to cause all things to be added to their life; as they prove faithful with what God has given to them, they will be exalted; as they delight in the Lord, He gives them the desires of their hearts.

In conclusion, make your life easier by loving God with all of your heart and your neighbor as yourself.

Developing a Prosperous Soul
Vol. I: How to Overcome a Poverty Mind-set
Vol. II: How to Move into God's Financial Blessings

There are fundamental changes you can make in the way you think which will release God's blessings. This is a balanced look at God's promises with practical steps you can take to move into financial freedom. It is time for Christians to recapture the financial arena.

Spiritual Realities

(Now five volumes* of a seven volume series)

Here they are—the series explaining the spiritual world from a Christian perspective. In this series Harold R. Eberle deals with issues such as:

- What exists in the spiritual world
- Discerning things in the spirit
- Interpretation of dreams
- Angelic and demonic visitations
- Activities of witches, psychics and New Agers
- The Christian perspective of holistic medicine
- Spiritual impartations and influences between people
- Understanding supernatural phenomena from a Biblical perspective

- How people access that realm
- Out-of-the-body experiences
- What the dead are experiencing

Now you can have answers to the questions you always have wanted to ask about the supernatural world and spiritual phenomena.

Vol. I: The Spiritual World and How We Access It
Vol. II: The Breath of God in Us
Vol. III: Escaping Dualism

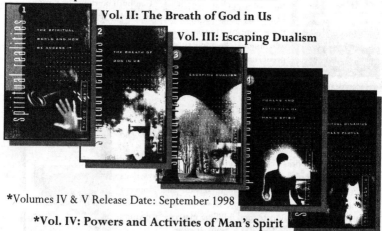

*Volumes IV & V Release Date: September 1998
*Vol. IV: Powers and Activities of Man's Spirit
*Vol. V: Spiritual Dynamics Between People

People Are Good

Harold R. Eberle is stirring up controversy with this one. Furthering the present reformation within the Church this book will cause a major paradigm shift in your mind. It will challenge fundamental beliefs, yet set Christians free and rejoicing. After reading this book you will look at life differently—more positively, with more hope and more realistically. You never will be the same.

You Shall Receive Power

Moving Beyond Pentecostal & Charismatic Theology

God's Spirit will fill you in measures beyond what you are experiencing presently. This is not about Pentecostal or Charismatic blessings. There is something greater. It is for all Christians and it will build a bridge between those Christians who speak in tongues and those who do not. It is time for the whole Church to take a fresh look at the work of the Holy Spirit in our individual lives. This book will help you. It will challenge you, broaden your perspective, set you rejoicing, fill you with hope, and leave you longing for more of God.

Dear Pastors and Traveling Ministers,

Here is a manual to help pastors and traveling ministers relate and minister together effectively. Topics are addressed such as finances, authority, ethical concerns, scheduling,.... In addition to dealing with real-life situations, an appendix is included with very practical worksheets to offer traveling ministers and local pastors a means to communicate with each other. Pastors and traveling ministers can make their lives and work much easier simply by reading this manual.